THE
TRAVELLER'S
POCKET BIBLE

THE
TRAVELLER'S
POCKET BIBLE

EVERY TRAVELLING RULE OF THUMB
AT YOUR FINGERTIPS

PAUL JENNER &
CHRISTINE SMITH

WHITE
LADDER
PRESS
new tricks for old dogs

The Traveller's Pocket Bible

This edition first published in Great Britain 2008 by
Crimson Publishing, a division of Crimson Business Ltd
Westminster House
Kew Road
Richmond
Surrey
TW9 2ND

A catalogue record for this book is available from the British library.

ISBN 978 1 905410 46 0

Designed and typeset by Julie Martin Ltd
Cover design by Julie Martin Ltd
Printed in the UK by CPI William Clowes Beccles NR34 7TL

CONTENTS

INTRODUCTION

Will you be able to plug in your mobile phone charger in Barcelona? Will you be able to plug your laptop into the telephone socket in New York? What jabs should you have for a trip to Morocco? Is that perfume in the airport shop really a bargain? How can you get the cheapest flight to Bangkok or the best-value hotel room in Paris?

These, and hundreds more questions, are answered in *The Traveller's Pocket Bible*.

We're all of us travelling far more than we used to and are far more sophisticated about foreign countries than we used to be. But, if anything, in our increasingly complicated world, the number of questions just keeps multiplying.

Whether you travel a great deal, whether you travel once a year or whether you're planning your first ever trip abroad, *The Traveller's Pocket Bible* gives you all the answers at your fingertips. It could save you a lot of money. And a lot of problems and frustration, too.

We've been all over the world in our work as travel writers. One thing we lacked was a little book we could slip into a pocket that would remind us about all those elusive but vital bits of travel information. We never found one. So we've written one.

We hope you find it useful.

Paul Jenner and Christine Smith
Catalonia, 2008

ACCOMMODATION

✳ HOTELS ✳

Anyone walking into a hotel, or telephoning, to ask for a room will be quoted the 'walk in' price or 'rack rate'. That also happens to be the highest price. However, what you want is the 'corporate rate', the rate paid by companies that do business regularly with the hotel, or, better still, the 'preferred rate', an even cheaper rate for companies doing large amounts of business with the hotel.

One way to get a reduction is to use an internet booking company such as:

➤ www.bedbookers.com
➤ www.expedia.com
➤ www.expotel.co.uk
➤ www.go2spain.co.uk (Spain only)
➤ www.hotelpronto.com
➤ www.hotels.co.uk
➤ www.laterooms.com
➤ www.octopustravel.com
➤ www.superbreak.com (short breaks)
➤ www.travelocity.com

NAME YOUR PRICE

The website www.priceline.co.uk has a system in which you

literally 'name your price'. The idea is that you select the town, city or area of the city you require together with the star-rating you want and then make an offer of the price you're willing to pay. Quite often, if a hotel has empty rooms, you'll get a bargain. But remember that by initiating the search you're committing yourself to whichever hotel accepts the booking (if one does) and your credit card will be debited, whether you like the hotel or not.

Expert's tip ✦

If you arrive in a city without having booked a hotel go into the nearest large travel agent and ask if they can book a hotel for you. Many of the travel agency chains have special arrangements with hotels and should be able to get a much lower price than you can. Of course, the agent takes a commission from the hotel so, in theory, if you're good at negotiating (see below), you should be able to get an even lower price – but in reality you probably won't.

WHAT'S THE HOTEL LIKE?

The hotel's website should give you a pretty good idea but to get an independent opinion try www.tripadvisor.com.

CLUBS

www.iapa.com – Members of the International Airline Passengers Association enjoy a range of benefits including discounts on hotels. Membership costs £69/€99.

www.travel-offers.co.uk 0871 282 2882 has two different clubs. For an annual membership fee of £29.95 you and a partner can stay free as many times as you like at some 320 UK hotels, provided you pay for dinner and breakfast (typically ranging in price from £23.50 up to £49 each). Or, for an annual membership of £28.50 you can save up to 50% off the B&B price of 130 hotels.

www.theaa.com – Membership of the AA entitles you to discounts at various hotels.

NEGOTIATING

There's no point in trying to negotiate with Central Reservations because they usually can't offer discounts (except as part of some advertised promotion). But if you enjoy negotiating and are good at it try some of the following directly with the hotel:

➤ Phone the hotel at different times to see if you can get a better rate from a different staff member.

➤ If you intend to stay several nights in a city including a Sunday night, book the Sunday night on its own first. Few city hotels are busy on a Sunday night so you'll probably get a good rate. Then, later, call to add the other days – which, hopefully, you'll get at the same price.

➤ Always ask for a non-smoking room and say you'll pay by credit card – hotels find that smokers who pay cash are the most troublesome.

STOPOVERS

If you're flying in and out with the same airline your carrier should be able to get a discount for you on selected hotels.

'FAST' HOTELS

Some of the same principles applied to fast food chains have been adapted for hotels. They're purpose-built using lots of prefabrication, usually situated on the outskirts of large towns on factory estates, and run by a tiny staff. At the very cheapest you might, for example, gain access to the building and to a room using a credit card without ever seeing a receptionist. As with fast food chains you get an inexpensive product in modern surroundings and with a good standard of cleanliness.

Expert's tip ✛

Have pen and paper handy if there's an automated check-in at your fast hotel – the screen will show a code which you'll have to remember for access to the main door and to your room.

➤ www.hotelformule1.com – Mostly in France but also hotels in the UK, Belgium, the Netherlands, Sweden, Germany, Switzerland, Spain, Australia, South Africa, Brazil and Japan.

➤ www.premiereclasse.com – Mostly France but also hotels in the UK, Italy, Luxembourg, the Netherlands, Poland, Portugal and Spain. Also on your mobile phone at www.premiereclasse.mobi

➤ www.kyriad.com – Mostly France but also hotels in the UK, Italy, Luxembourg, the Netherlands, Poland, Portugal and Spain.

➤ www.bonsai-hotel.tm.fr – France only.

➤ www.comfortinn.com – Worldwide, slightly more expensive chain embracing several brands in the USA, Canada, UK, Europe, Australasia, Asia, the Caribbean and South America.

➤ www.balladins.com – Some 160 slightly more expensive hotels in France and Belgium.

➤ www.campanile.com – Slightly more expensive hotels in France, the UK, Italy, Luxembourg, the Netherlands, Poland, Portugal and Spain.

➤ www.daysinn.com – Mostly USA but also worldwide.

➤ www.premierinn.com – UK's largest chain of budget hotels.

➤ www.travelodge.co.uk – Probably the UK's cheapest chain of hotels.

✳ SELF-CATERING ✳ ACCOMMODATION

Self-catering accommodation is increasingly popular and not merely with those who can't afford hotels. (Indeed, some luxury apartments and houses can be even more expensive.) Advantages include space, the convenience of being able to make drinks, snacks and meals whenever you want, the fun of buying food at local markets and the ability (in some cases) to get right away from overcrowded tourist spots. To track down what you want put 'self-catering' or 'holiday rent' into your search engine together with the name of your destination, or try one of the following websites:

➤ www.holidaylets.net
➤ www.holiday-rentals.co.uk
➤ www.homelidays.com
➤ www.landmarktrust.org.uk
➤ www.ownersdirect.co.uk

✳ CAMPING AND CARAVANNING ✳

Put 'campsite' into your search engine together with the name of your destination or take a look at:

➤ www.eurocampings.net
➤ www.europe-camping-guide.com
➤ www.interhike.com
➤ www.ukcampsite.co.uk

2

COMMUNICATIONS

Keeping in touch from abroad has never been easier but it can, nevertheless, be extremely expensive. Ideally you should check out all the options in good time before you go and make the necessary arrangements. But even if you haven't done so there are still various low-cost arrangements you can make while travelling.

✳ MOBILES ✳

Here are a few tips about using your mobile abroad:

➢ Ask your UK mobile network provider to enable your phone for international roaming. At the same time, ask for the full number of your voicemail box (the short dial number used in the UK may not work abroad).

➢ Check the cost of calls to see if it's worth switching to a different tariff – for example, it may be best to pay a monthly fee so that calls abroad are cheaper.

➢ Make sure you know what codes you have to dial when using your phone abroad.

➢ Programme in emergency numbers such as the nearest British embassy or consulate, your hotel, your tour operator and so on.

➢ Make sure you have your phone charger with you, together

with an appropriate adaptor. If you're going to a country where the voltage is significantly different (the USA, for example) make sure you have a charger that can handle the lower current.

➤ Make a note of the phone's IMEI (serial number), the number of your operator's customer services department, and the mobile's telephone number so that you can have the phone/SIM blocked in case of theft.

➤ Four different mobile phone frequencies are in use worldwide. They are 850MHz, 900 MHz, 1800 MHz and 1900 MHz. If you want to be able to use a mobile phone anywhere in the world you therefore need a **quad-band** model.

➤ To save money, ask people to text you rather than telephone. You may prefer not to answer calls so you can pick messages up later from voicemail.

➤ For other ways of saving money see below.

✳ CHEAP CALLS ABROAD ✳

➤ www.vyke.com – Vyke has several products to cut the cost of your calls while abroad (and at home). They include Vyke Callback (you dial a special number and then are called back) and the ability to make calls from your laptop, virtually free.

➤ www.1st4phonecard.com – Phone card producers can buy time in bulk from line carriers at huge savings. On international calls discounts can be as high as 80% and sometimes even more. The phone card companies keep a margin for themselves and pass the rest on to you. You buy a prepaid 'card` (in some cases, it's just an internet receipt) and then you can make cheap calls from any touch tone phone, simply by dialling an access code and then entering a PIN number.

This site compares rates from the various phone card companies so you can get the best deal.

> A new local/global SIM card for your mobile. You swap your normal SIM for one from a discount company. You can buy global cards that cover you in almost any country or you can buy a SIM specific to just one country. Pricing structures vary so it's best to compare several for the destination or destinations you plan to visit and the level of calls you expect. Put 'international SIM card' into your internet search engine. Companies to consider include www.sim4travel.net, www.0044.co.uk, www.oneroam.co.uk and www.global simcard.co.uk.

Expert's tip ✦

If, for whatever reason, you don't have a mobile with you, you can rent one for the duration of your stay in most large cities and popular tourist destinations. But check on the internet beforehand – for some destinations it may be easier to rent in the UK before you go.

VoIP

VoIP stands for Voice over Internet Protocol. Skype, the best-known operator, prefers the easier tag of 'free calls over the internet'. It works with both dial-up and broadband connections. As long as you and the person you're calling are both registered for Skype then it's completely free. All you – and your contacts – have to do is download the software at www.skype.com.

A variation is to use the internet to route calls via ordinary landlines or mobile technology. You enter the number via your laptop but you actually speak on your telephone. This system is provided by www.jajah.co.uk. Calls between Jajah registered users on landlines are free in Europe, Australia, New Zealand and

Taiwan. At the moment, free mobile calls are only possible in the USA, Canada, China, Singapore and Hong Kong. Note that, although the call is free, your hotel may nevertheless add something.

✳ USING YOUR LAPTOP ABROAD ✳

Before travelling with your laptop:

➤ Check to see if you have an international warranty and what you should do if the laptop either malfunctions or is stolen.

➤ Protect it with a purpose-designed case – choose a model that doesn't make it obvious there's a valuable laptop inside.

Most laptops are dual voltage and can be used anywhere but, just to be sure, check that yours is. If not, you'll need an appropriate transformer to use your laptop in a country which has a different voltage.

You'll also need:

➤ An adaptor for the electrical socket.

➤ An adaptor for the telephone socket – for suppliers see Appendix 2.

Expert's tip ✛

Phone outlets in some hotels may not be suitable for modems. You can check by using a modem saver, which is a kind of test lamp. Just insert the modem saver into the socket and the colour of the lamp will indicate whether or not it's safe to use.

And, of course, you'll need an account you can use abroad:

METHOD 1. Open an account with a company such as CompuServe

(http://webcenters.netscape.compuserve.com) which then allows you access via a local call anywhere in the world.

METHOD 2. Open an account with www.ipass.com. The company has negotiated dial-up services in some 160 countries as well as hotel Ethernet broadband and around 90,000 Wi-Fi hotspots in some 70 countries (see below). It means you can use your laptop in just about every popular destination. Wherever you are, you simply log-in and then click on the nearest suitable connection. The website www.btopenzone.com sells international Wi-Fi vouchers that can be used on the Continent and many countries worldwide.

USING WI-FI

Expert's tip ✦
- Before you go, back-up your data on, say, a memory stick and leave it in a safe place. Also back up data while travelling and keep the memory device separate from the laptop.
- Take your laptop as hand luggage on the aircraft; keep it with you at all times.
- Insure your laptop for travel.

Almost all recent laptops will have Wi-Fi built in, which means that if you're in a Wi-Fi hotspot you can connect to the internet without a cable. If your laptop doesn't have Wi-Fi you can have it installed. Some hotspots are free but usually you'll have to pay.

To seek out hotspots in your planned destinations go to www.jiwire.com/search-hotspot-locations.htm. The site currently lists some 221,000 in 135 countries.

If you haven't used a hotspot before, this is how it works:

➤ Try to find a place within the hotspot where the signal is strongest (the range is normally about 100m); if you're not sure, ask.

➤ Open your laptop and turn it on.

➤ If you have a physical switch to turn on Wi-Fi, then turn that on as well.

➤ Look for the little screen icon that depicts a computer screen with three waves coming out of it.

➤ Right click on the icon and select 'View Available Wireless Networks'.

➤ Look for the SSID (the access point name) that corresponds with the hotspot provider for your location (there may be a sticker on the window that tells you the name).

➤ Select the SSID and click 'Connect'.

➤ Open your browser.

➤ A log-in screen will then appear. If it's a subscription hotspot, enter your identification including your password; if it's a free hotspot enter the details requested.

➤ You are now ready to do what you want.

WI-FI SECURITY

When you're using a hotspot the data you're sending and receiving isn't secure. A criminal could intercept your passwords and logins, as well as your messages, with devastating effect. The solution is to erect a firewall and encrypt data. Both of these services are available at www.jiwire.com.

Expert's tip ✦

♦ It sometimes happens that you are apparently connected at a Wi-Fi hotspot, and being charged, but you can't download any data. If this happens disconnect immediately and try a different position or different Wi-Fi service.

♦ Make sure you log off correctly, otherwise you may continue to be charged until automatically disconnected due to inactivity (generally 15 minutes).

✳ SATELLITE PHONES ✳

If you're travelling in an area without either a fixed-line telephone service or mobile coverage, satellite phones are now an affordable option. Technology has reduced the cost of calls as well as the size of the handset and antenna. However, they are not competitive where ordinary mobile phone coverage is available. For short periods, satellite phones can be rented.

The main systems are:

➤ Iridium – global.

➤ Inmarsat – three levels of which the most comprehensive is global but excluding the polar regions.

➤ Globalstar – Americas, Europe, North African coast, Russia, Middle East, Australia, New Zealand.

➤ Thuraya – Europe, North Africa, Middle East, India.

All support emails but Inmarsat is much faster than the others. Only Iridium and Thuraya support SMS messages.

Expert's tip ✦

If you want to use a satellite phone inside a building or vehicle you'll need an external aerial because they require a clear line of site to the satellite.

Companies selling and renting satellite phones include:

➤ www.satphone.co.uk 0800 747 6 747
➤ http://satcomms.com 01493 440 011
➤ www.mobell.co.uk 0800 24 35 24

✳ TELEPHONE SOCKETS ✳

Although the number of Wi-Fi locations is growing rapidly all over the world, sometimes you may still need to plug your laptop into a telephone socket. The good news is that there aren't quite as many types of telephone socket as there are electric sockets. In fact, most of the world uses a standard known as RJ11. The bad news is that in the UK, unless you're on the high-speed system known as ADSL, you'll be using a completely different standard known as BS 6312. When you go abroad you'll therefore need an adaptor for most destinations.

YOUR COMPLETE GUIDE TO TELEPHONE SOCKETS AROUND THE WORLD

Most of the world, including Canada and the USA	RJ11
Austria	TDO
Belgium	Tetrapolar
Botswana	BS 6312
Brazil	Telebrás or RJ11
Cyprus	BS 6312 with RJ11 for ADSL
Denmark	Danish 3-prong except for recent RJ11 installations
France	F-010

Germany	TAE (or RJ45 for ISDN lines)
Gibraltar	BS 6312
Liechtenstein	Reichle connectors
Morocco	F-010
New Zealand	BS 6312
Switzerland	Reichle connectors
UAE	BS 6312
UK	BS 6312 (but RJ11 for ADSL)

Expert's tip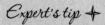

Don't rely on being able to buy a telephone adaptor at the airport. They can be difficult to find. Order one well before you're due to leave.

3

CONVERSION TABLES

✳ CURRENCY QUICK CONVERTER ✳

The following rules of thumb will give you an *approximate* idea of foreign prices converted into pounds sterling. Remember that currencies can fluctuate and these methods are no more than a rough indication. If you're interested in buying something use a calculator and the latest exchange rate to arrive at an accurate conversion.

FOREIGN CURRENCY INTO POUNDS STERLING (APPROXIMATE)

➤ Baht (Thai) into pounds – divide by 10 and then divide by 6

➤ Dollars (US, Canadian or Australian) into pounds – divide by 2

➤ Dollars (New Zealand) – multiply by 4 then knock off the last digit

➤ Dollars (Hong Kong) into pounds – divide by 10 and then subtract one-third.

➤ Euros into pounds – divide by 5 and multiply by 4

➤ Franc (Swiss) into pounds – divide by 2

➤ Krona (Swedish) into pounds – halve it, halve it again, then divide by 3

➤ Krone (Danish) into pounds – divide by 10

➤ Krone (Norwegian) into pounds – divide by 10

➤ Lire (Turkish) into pounds – divide by 2 and then subtract 10%

➤ Rand (South African) into pounds – divide by 10 and then subtract one-third

➤ Rupees (Indian) into pounds – divide by 10, then halve it, halve it again, and halve it again.

POUNDS STERLING INTO FOREIGN CURRENCY

➤ Pounds into baht (Thai) – add a 0 and multiply by 6

➤ Pounds into dollars (US, Canadian or Australian) – multiply by 2

➤ Pounds into dollars (New Zealand) – add a 0 then divide by 4

➤ Pounds into dollars (Hong Kong) – add a 0 and then increase the figure by half as much again.

➤ Pounds into euros – divide by 4 and multiply by 5

➤ Pounds into francs (Swiss) – multiply by 2

➤ Pounds into krona (Swedish) – add a 0 and then add another fifth

➤ Pounds into krone (Danish) – multiply by 10

➤ Pounds into krone (Norwegian) – multiply by 10

➤ Pounds into lire (Turkish) – multiply by 2 and then increase the result by 10%

➤ Pounds into rand (South African) - add a 0 and then increase the figure by half as much again.

➤ Pounds into rupees (Indian) – double it, double it again, double it again, and then add a 0.

Expert's tip ✦

Round the figure up or down to make the calculation easier. Example: if something costs 98 euros round it up to 100 euros so you can more easily divide it by 5. Remember, you're only estimating – for an accurate figure use a calculator and the latest exchange rate. Or use an online calculator such as:

♦ *www.x-rates.com*

✳ DISTANCE ✳

METRIC TO IMPERIAL

➤ 1 millimetre = 0.03937 inch
➤ 10 millimetres = 1 centimetre = 0.3937 inch
➤ 100 centimetres = 1 metre = 39.37 inches = 3.2808 feet
➤ 1,000 metres = 1 kilometre = 3280.8 feet = 0.621 miles

❘ *Rule of thumb* ☼

For an approximate conversion of kilometres to miles divide by 8 and multiply by 5.

IMPERIAL TO METRIC

➤ 1 inch = 2.54 centimetres
➤ 12 inches = 1 foot = 0.3048 metres

➤ 3 feet = 1 yard = 0.9144 metre

➤ 5280 feet = 1760 yards = 1 mile = 1.6093 kilometres

Rule of thumb ☀

For an approximate conversion of miles to kilometres divide by 5 and multiply by 8.

✳ AREA ✳

METRIC TO IMPERIAL

➤ 1 square metre = 1549.9 square inches = 1.196 square yards

➤ 1 hectare = 2.471 acres

➤ 100 hectares = 1 square kilometre = 247.1 acres = 0.386 square miles

IMPERIAL TO METRIC

1 square yard = 9 square feet = 0.8361 square metre

1 acre = 0.4047 hectare

Rule of thumb ☀

- *For an approximate conversion of hectares to acres multiply by 5 and divide by 2.*
- *For an approximate conversion of square kilometres to square miles multiply by four and divide by 10.*

➤ 1 square mile = 640 acres = 2.59 square kilometres = 259 hectares

Rule of thumb ☀

For an approximate conversion of acres to hectares multiply by 2

and divide by 5.
For an approximate conversion of square miles to square
kilometres multiply by 10 and divide by 4.

✳ WEIGHT ✳

METRIC TO IMPERIAL

➤ 1 gram = 0.035274 ounce
➤ 1 kilogram = 2.2046 pounds
➤ 1 metric ton = 2204.6 pounds = 0.9842 imperial ton

Rule of thumb ☼

- *For an approximate conversion of kilograms to pounds multiply*
  by 2 and then add another 10% (5 kilograms = 5 x 2
  pounds + 10% = 10 pounds + 1 pound = 11 pounds).
- *Metric and imperial tons are approximately the same.*

IMPERIAL TO METRIC

➤ 1 ounce = 28.3495 grams
➤ 1 pound = 453.59 grams = 0.45359 kilogram
➤ 1 imperial ton = 1016.05 kilograms = 1.01605 metric tons

✳ LIQUIDS ✳

Rule of thumb ☼

- *For an approximate conversion of pounds to kilograms subtract*
  10% and then divide by 2.
- *Imperial and metric tons are approximately the same.*

METRIC TO IMPERIAL

➤ 1 litre = 1.76 pints

Rule of thumb ☼

1 standard bottle of wine = 6 standard glasses; 1 litre of wine = 8 standard glasses.
3 litres of beer is roughly equivalent to 5 pints.

IMPERIAL TO METRIC

➤ 1 pint = 20 fluid ounces = 0.568 litre

➤ 1 gallon = 4.546 litres

✳ TEMPERATURE ✳

Fahrenheit	32	40	50	60	70	80	90	100
Centigrade	0	4.4	10	15.6	21.1	26.7	32.2	37.8

Rule of thumb ☼

- *To convert Centigrade to Fahrenheit divide by 5, multiply by 9 and add 32. Example: 25°C = (25 ÷ 5) × 9 + 32 = (5 × 9) + 32 = 45 + 32 = 77°F.*
- *To convert Fahrenheit to Centigrade subtract 32, divide by 9 and multiply by 5. Example: 86°F = (86 – 32) ÷ 9 × 5 = (54 ÷ 9) × 5 = 6 × 5 = 30°C.*

4

ELECTRICITY

Broadly speaking, the world is divided into two standards for voltage and frequency but there are about a dozen different kinds of plugs/sockets.

✳ VOLTAGE AND FREQUENCY ✳

The UK electricity supply is 230 volts at a frequency of 50 Hz and most of the world is the same. The only *popular* destinations that operate a different standard are the USA and Canada, where the supply is 120 volts at 60 Hz, and parts of the Caribbean. To operate UK electrical equipment in these destinations you'll need either a converter or a transformer, to step down the current, as well as an adaptor for the socket.

Expert's tip ✛

If you don't know the voltage where you are take a look at a light bulb. The voltage will be printed on it somewhere.

CONVERTERS

Converters are simple devices for either stepping up or down the voltage but they can only be used with heaters and mechanical motors – hairdryers, toothbrushes and so on. They can't be used with electronic devices (that is, those with chips) nor can they be used for long periods. Don't leave a converter plugged in when not in use.

TRANSFORMERS

Transformers are more sophisticated than converters and work on a different principle. They can be used with electronic equipment that contains a chip – CD players, camcorder battery rechargers, radios, TVs and so on – as well as less-sophisticated electrical equipment.

CHOOSING A TRANSFORMER

The wattage rating of the transformer must be at least 25% greater than that of the appliance. Therefore, to run a small 75 watt CD player you'll need a transformer rated at, say, 100 watts. If you intend to run several appliances at the same time you'll need to add all the wattages together and then allow a 25% margin.

Expert's tip ✦

The wattage of an appliance is usually marked on it somewhere. If only the voltage and amperage are given you can calculate the wattage by multiplying the two together – 230 volts x 2 amps = 460 watts.

50 HZ OR 60 HZ – WHAT DIFFERENCE DOES IT MAKE?

Not much usually. Most modern equipment will work just as well with 50 Hz as with 60 Hz. Occasionally, you may find that an electric motor runs faster or slower than intended and clocks may not keep time. For example, a mains-powered clock from the UK will gain several minutes an hour in the USA. From the technical viewpoint 60 Hz is far more efficient in terms of generation, transmission and usage but, nevertheless, most countries followed the lead set years ago by AEG and opted for 50 Hz.

ADAPTORS

An adaptor simply allows you to connect your existing plug with a different type of socket. However, if the voltage is different, too, you still won't be able to use your appliance. For that you'll additionally need either a converter or a transformer (see above).

At least a dozen different kinds of plugs/sockets may be encountered around the world. They are:

➤ TYPE A. Plugs have two flat parallel pins.

➤ TYPE B. Plugs have two flat parallel pins as in type A and an additional round earthing pin.

➤ TYPE C. Comes in several forms. The Europlug (CEE 7/16) has two round 4 mm pins spaced 19 mm apart and is used in most of continental Europe as well as the Middle East, Africa, much of South America, the former Soviet Republics and many developing countries. The German and French version (CEE 7/17) has two round 4.8 mm pins. In the UK and Ireland a version of the Type C is used as a shaver socket in bathrooms, requiring a plug with two 5mm pins set 16.6 mm apart.

➤ TYPE D. This is the old British plug with three round pins in a triangular pattern and is still in use in India and other parts of the world electrified by British companies.

➤ TYPE E. Plugs have two round 4.8 mm pins spaced 19 mm apart plus hole to accept the earth pin that projects from the socket. The socket will also accept the Type C Europlug and CEE 7/17 version (see above). This set-up is used France, Belgium, Poland, the Czech Republic, Slovakia and, since July 2008, Denmark.

➤ TYPE F. Popularly known as a 'Schuko plug' this is a German standard and is similar to type E with two 4.8 mm pins but earthed by clips on the sides of the plug. It's used in several other countries including Austria, Italy and Spain. A variant is used in the CIS but with 4mm pins.

➢ TYPE G. This is the British 13 amp square-pin plug and it is used in a few other countries including Bahrain, Cyprus, the Falkland Islands, Hong Kong, Ireland, Malaysia and Singapore.

➢ TYPE H. This set-up has three flat pins and is unique to Israel.

➢ TYPE I. The plug has two flat pins set at an angle as well as an earthing pin. It is used in Australia, Fiji, New Zealand and Papua New Guinea. A variant is used in China with pins 1mm longer – Australasian plugs can be used in China but Chinese plugs won't fit properly into Australasian sockets. Yet another variant is used in Argentina, where the live and neutral wires are reversed.

➢ TYPE J. This plug is used in Switzerland and, from 2009, is the only plug that can be sold with domestic appliances in Brazil. It is similar to the Europlug and, in fact, Swiss sockets can take Europlugs.

➢ TYPE K. A three-pin plug to a Danish standard. The Danish sockets will also accept Europlugs and type E French plugs.

➢ TYPE L. A three-pin design used in Italy and coming in 10 A and 16 A versions with different pin diameters and spacings.

➢ TYPE M. Similar to type D and used in South Africa.

YOUR COMPLETE GUIDE TO VOLTAGE, FREQUENCY AND
PLUG TYPE AROUND THE WORLD

Country	Voltage	Frequency	Plug Type
Afghanistan	220	50 Hz	C/F
Albania	230	50 Hz	C/F
Algeria	230	50 Hz	C/F
American Samoa	120	60 Hz	A/B/F/I
Andorra	230	50 Hz	C/F
Angola	220	50 Hz	C
Anguilla	110	60 Hz	A
Antigua	230	60 Hz	A/B
Argentina	220	50 Hz	C/I
Armenia	230	50 Hz	C/F
Aruba	120	60 Hz	A/B/F
Australia	240	50 Hz	I
Austria	230	50 Hz	C/F
Azerbaijan	220	50 Hz	C/F
Azores	230	50 Hz	B/C/F
Bahamas	120	60 Hz	A/B
Bahrain	230	60 Hz	G
Balearic Islands	230	50 Hz	C/F
Bangladesh	220	50 Hz	C/D/G/K
Barbados	115	50 Hz	A/B
Belarus	230	50 Hz	C/F
Belgium	230	50 Hz	E
Belize	110/220	60 Hz	B/G
Benin	220	50 Hz	E
Bermuda	120	60 Hz	A/B
Bhutan	230	50 Hz	D/F/G
Bolivia	230	50 Hz	A/C
Bosnia & Herzegovina	230	50 Hz	C/F
Botswana	230	50 Hz	D/G
Brazil	127/220*	60 Hz	A/B/C/I
Brunei	240	50 Hz	G
Bulgaria	230	50 Hz	C/F
Burkina Faso	220	50 Hz	C/E

Country	Voltage	Frequency	Plug Type
Burundi	220	50 Hz	C/E
Cambodia	230	50 Hz	A/C/G
Cameroon	220	50 Hz	C/E
Canada	120	60 Hz	A/B
Canary Islands	230	50 Hz	C/E/L
Cape Verde	230	50 Hz	C/F
Cayman Islands	120	60 Hz	A/B
Central African Republic	220	50 Hz	C/E
Chad	220	50 Hz	D/E/F
Channel Islands (Guernsey & Jersey)	230	50 Hz	C/G
Chile	220	50 Hz	C/L
China	220	50 Hz	A/G/I
Colombia	110	60 Hz	A/B
Comoros	220	50 Hz	C/E
Congo, People's Republic	230	50 Hz	C/E
Congo, Democratic Republic	220	50 Hz	C/D
Cook Islands	240	50 Hz	I
Costa Rica	120	60 Hz	A/B
Côte d'Ivoire	220	50 Hz	C/E
Croatia	230	50 Hz	C/F
Cuba	110/220	60 Hz	A/B/C/L
Cyprus	230	50 Hz	G/F**
Czech Republic	230	50 Hz	E
Denmark	230	50 Hz	C/F/K
Djibouti	220	50 Hz	C/E
Dominica	230	50 Hz	D/G
Dominican Republic	110	60 Hz	A/B
East Timor	220	50 Hz	C/E/F/I
Ecuador	110	60 Hz	A/B
Egypt	220	50 Hz	C/F
El Salvador	115	60 Hz	A/B/C/D/E/ F/G/I/J/L
Equatorial Guinea	220	50 Hz	C/E
Eritrea	230	50 Hz	C/L
Estonia	230	50 Hz	C/F

Country	Voltage	Frequency	Plug Type
Ethiopia	220	50 Hz	C/F
Faeroe Islands	230	50 Hz	C/K
Falkland Islands	240	50 Hz	G
Fiji	240	50 Hz	I
Finland	230	50 Hz	C/F
France	230	50 Hz	E
French Guyana	220	50 Hz	C/D/E
Gabon	220	50 Hz	C
Gambia	230	50 Hz	G
Gaza	230	50 Hz	H
Georgia	220	50 Hz	C/F
Germany	230	50 Hz	C/F
Ghana	230	50 Hz	D/G
Gibraltar	230	50 Hz	C/G
Greece	230	50 Hz	C/F
Greenland	230	50 Hz	C/K
Grenada (Windward Is.)	230	50 Hz	G
Guadeloupe	230	50 Hz	C/D/E
Guam	110	60 Hz	A/B
Guatemala	120	60 Hz	A/B/G/I
Guinea	220	50 Hz	C/F/K
Guinea-Bissau	220	50 Hz	C
Guyana	240	60 Hz	A/B/D/G
Haiti	110	60 Hz	A/B
Honduras	110	60 Hz	A/B
Hong Kong	220	50 Hz	G
Hungary	230	50 Hz	C/F
Iceland	230	50 Hz	C/F
India	230	50 Hz	C/D/M
Indonesia	230	50 Hz	C/F
Iran	230	50 Hz	C/F
Iraq	230	50 Hz	C/D/G
Ireland	230	50 Hz	G
Isle of Man	230	50 Hz	C/G
Israel	230	50 Hz	H/C

Country	Voltage	Frequency	Plug Type
Italy	230	50 Hz	C/F/L
Jamaica	110	50 Hz	A/B
Japan	100	50/60 Hz**	A/B
Jordan	230	50 Hz	C/D/F/G/J
Kenya	240	50 Hz	G
Kazakhstan	220	50 Hz	C/F
Kiribati	240	50 Hz	I
Korea, North	110/220	60 Hz	A/C
Korea, South	110/220	60 Hz	A/B/C/F
Kuwait	240	50 Hz	C/G
Kyrgyzstan	220	50 Hz	C/F
Laos	230	50 Hz	A/B/C/E/F
Latvia	230	50 Hz	C/F
Lebanon	230	50 Hz	C/D/G
Lesotho	220	50 Hz	M
Liberia	120	60 Hz	A/B
Libya	127/230	50 Hz	D/F
Liechtenstein	230	50 Hz	J
Lithuania	230	50 Hz	C/F
Luxembourg	230	50 Hz	C/F
Macau	220	50 Hz	D/G
Macedonia	230	50 Hz	C/F
Madagascar	127/220	50 Hz	C/D/E/J/K
Madeira	230	50 Hz	C/F
Malawi	230	50 Hz	G
Malaysia	240	50 Hz	G
Maldives	230	50 Hz	D/G/J/K/L
Mali	220	50 Hz	C/E
Malta	230	50 Hz	G
Martinique	220	50 Hz	C/D/E
Mauritania	220	50 Hz	C
Mauritius	230	50 Hz	C/G
Mexico	127	60 Hz	A
Micronesia	120	60 Hz	A/B
Moldova	230	50 Hz	C/F

Country	Voltage	Frequency	Plug Type
Monaco	230	50 Hz	C/D/E/F
Mongolia	230	50 Hz	C/E
Montenegro	230	50 Hz	C/F
Montserrat (Leeward Is.)	230	60 Hz	A/B
Morocco	220	50 Hz	C/E
Mozambique	220	50 Hz	C/F/M
Myanmar	230	50 Hz	C/D/F/G
Namibia	220	50 Hz	D/M
Nauru	240	50 Hz	I
Nepal	230	50 Hz	C/D/M
Netherlands	230	50 Hz	C/F
Netherlands Antilles	127/220	50 Hz	A/B/F
New Caledonia	220	50 Hz	F
New Zealand	240	50 Hz	I
Nicaragua	120	60 Hz	A
Niger	220	50 Hz	A/B/C/D/E/F
Nigeria	230	50 Hz	D/G
Norway	230	50 Hz	C/F
Oman	240	50 Hz	C/G
Pakistan	230	50 Hz	C/D
Palau	120	60 Hz	A/B
Panama	110	60 Hz	A/B
Papua New Guinea	240	50 Hz	I
Paraguay	220	50 Hz	C
Peru	220	60 Hz	A/B/C
Philippines	220	60 Hz	A/B/C
Poland	230	50 Hz	C/E
Portugal	230	50 Hz	C/F
Puerto Rico	120	60 Hz	A/B
Qatar	240	50 Hz	D/G
Reunion	230	50 Hz	E
Romania	230	50 Hz	C/F
Russian Federation	230	50 Hz	C/F
Rwanda	230	50 Hz	C/J
St Kitts and Nevis	230	60 Hz	D/G

Country	Voltage	Frequency	Plug Type
St Lucia (Windward Is.)	230	50 Hz	G
St Vincent (Windward is.)	230	50 Hz	A/C/E/G/I/K
San Marino	230	50 Hz	F/L
Saudi Arabia	110/ 220***	60 Hz	A/B/C/G
Senegal	230	50 Hz	C/D/E/K
Serbia	230	50 Hz	C/F
Seychelles	240	50 Hz	G
Sierra Leone	230	50 Hz	D/G
Singapore	230	50 Hz	G
Slovakia	230	50 Hz	E
Slovenia	230	50 Hz	C/F
Somalia	220	50 Hz	C
South Africa	230	50 Hz	D/M***
Spain (ex. Canary Is.)	230	50 Hz	C/F
Sri Lanka	230	50 Hz	D/G/M
Sudan	230	50 Hz	C/D
Suriname	127	60 Hz	C/F
Swaziland	230	50 Hz	M
Sweden	230	50 Hz	C/F
Switzerland	230	50 Hz	J
Syria	220	50 Hz	C/E/L
Tahiti	220	50/60 Hz****	C/E
Tajikistan	220	50 Hz	C/F
Taiwan	110	60 Hz	A/B
Tanzania	230	50 Hz	D/G
Thailand	220	50 Hz	A/B/C
Togo	220	50 Hz	C
Tonga	240	50 Hz	I
Trinidad & Tobago	115	60 Hz	A/B
Tunisia	230	50 Hz	C/E
Turkey	230	50 Hz	C/F
Turkmenistan	220	50 Hz	C/F
Uganda	240	50 Hz	G
Ukraine	230	50 Hz	C/F

Country	Voltage	Frequency	Plug Type
United Arab Emirates	240	50 Hz	G
UK	230	50 Hz	G
USA	120	60 Hz	A/B
Uruguay	220	50 Hz	C/F/I/L
Uzbekistan	220	50 Hz	C/F
Venezuela	120	60 Hz	A/B
Vietnam	220	50 Hz	A/C/G
Virgin Islands	110	60 Hz	A/B
Western Samoa	230	50 Hz	I
Yemen	230	50 Hz	A/D/G
Zambia	230	50 Hz	C/D/G
Zimbabwe	240	50 Hz	D/G

NOTES:

* In Brazil the following states use 127 volts – Acre, Amapá, Amazonas, Bahia, Espírito Santo, Rio de Janeiro, Sao Paulo, Mato Grosso do Sul, Maranhao, Pará, Paraná, Rio Grande do Sul, Rondônia, Roraima, Sergipe, Minas Gerais (except the cities of Bagé, Caxias do Sul, Jequié, Jundiaí, Novo Friburgo, Pelotas, Santos, and Sao Bernardo do Campo, which use 220 volts). The following states use 220 volts – Alagoas, Brasília, Ceará, Mato Grosso, Goiás, Paraíba, Pernambuco, Piauí, Rio Grande do Norte, Santa Catarina, and Tocantins (except the cities of Paulista and Teresina which use 127 volts).

** Eastern Japan (Tokyo, Kawasaki, Sapporo, Yokohama, Sendai) mostly uses 50 Hz whereas Western Japan (Osaka, Kyoto, Nagoya, Hiroshima mostly uses 60 Hz).

*** 110 volts is the more widely used in Saudi Arabia but 220 volts is quite common, too, especially in hotels.

**** The frequency is 60 Hz except for the Marquesas where it's 50 Hz.

5

EMERGENCIES

✳ WHAT TO DO IF YOUR PASSPORT ✳ IS LOST OR STOLEN

STEP 1. Report the loss to the local police and receive a copy of the report with the crime reference details. Note that although the copy of the police form may be accepted as a kind of temporary passport in some countries it won't be accepted by airlines for international flights.

STEP 2. Report the loss to the nearest British Foreign and Commonwealth office, embassy, consulate or high commission, where you will be required to complete form LS01, including the crime reference details obtained from the police. You can also apply for replacement travel documents to get you back to the UK. To find your nearest FCO post call +44 20 7008 1500 or, if you have access to a computer, go to www.fco.gov.uk.

STEP 3. Once back in the UK apply for a replacement passport (the stolen passport will have been cancelled to prevent anyone else using it).

Things a British embassy, consulate or high commission may be able to do for you:

✓ Issue replacement travel documents

✓ Give advice about transferring money

✓ Give advice about finding local interpreters, lawyers, doctors and funeral directors

✓ Contact family or friends

✓ Give support if you are the victim of a serious crime or are in hospital

✓ Visit/contact you if you have been detained by the police

Things a British embassy, consulate or high commission will not do for you:

✗ Pay your bills or provide you with money, except in the most exceptional circumstances.

NOTE: You may be charged for some services and in the event of any money being advanced you will be required to pay it back.

✳ WHAT TO DO IF YOUR AIRLINE ✳ TICKET IS LOST OR STOLEN

Conventional airline tickets (as opposed to E-tickets) are somewhat like cash. Lose them and you may well have lost your money for good. It all depends on the airline's general conditions of carriage. Just because your name is in the airline computer it doesn't mean you can travel anyway. The problem is that whoever stole your ticket (or finds it) may be able to use it or cash it in (depending on the type of ticket). Here's what you should do:

STEP 1. Notify the theft or loss to the police and get a copy of the report.

STEP 2. Notify the airline. Most airlines will issue a replacement ticket if (a) you can provide proof that you had a ticket and (b)

you sign an indemnity in case the lost/stolen ticket is misused. If you cannot provide proof you had a ticket or you aren't willing to sign the indemnity then you'll be asked to pay the current price for a replacement (rather than the price you originally paid). In that case, once the validity period of the ticket has expired without it being misused, the airline will give you a refund.

STEP 3. If the airline doesn't offer a replacement, and you don't want to or can't pay out for one, go to the airport on the day of the flight and ask the airline ticket desk for one. Some do have this power in the case of hardship. You'll need to present your identification, a copy of the ticket if you have one, or at least the number, and a copy of the police report. You may be asked to pay an administration fee and sign an indemnity in case your stolen/lost ticket is used.

An E-ticket print-out, by contrast, is nothing more than a confirmation and therefore its loss is not serious. The actual ticket exists only in the airline computer and you can still travel without your printed confirmation. However, if you lost your passport at the same time you should inform the airline in case someone tries to travel using it.

WHAT TO DO IF YOUR CREDIT/
✳ DEBIT CARDS OR TRAVELLER'S ✳
CHEQUES ARE STOLEN

If you subscribe to a credit card protection service you can cancel all your cards with just one phone call. Membership may also confer various other benefits such as an emergency cash advance and payment of your hotel bill (see the chapter on Money for more details). If you don't have such a service you'll need to call each of your card companies individually. Here are the numbers:

Abbey (and Cahoot)
In the UK: 08459 724 724 option 3
From abroad: + 44 1908 237 963

Allied Irish Bank
In Ireland: 01668 5500
From abroad: + 353 1668 5500

Alliance & Leicester
Credit cards:
In the UK: 0800 0688 638
From abroad: + 44 1244 673 700
Current account cards/cheque books:
In the UK: 0500 31 32 33
From abroad: + 44 151 928 4033

American Express
Cards:
In the UK: 01273 696 933
From abroad: + 44 1273 696 933
Traveller's cheques:
In the UK: 0800 521 313
From abroad: + 44 1273 571 600

Bank of Ireland
In Ireland: 1890 706 706
From abroad: + 353 56 775 7007

Bank of Scotland
Credit cards:
In the UK: 0845 3000 344
Bank cards: 0845 7 20 30 99

Barclays Bank
In the UK: 01604 230 230
From abroad: + 44 1604 230 230

For those with Cardholder Protection:
In the UK: 0808 100 6667
From abroad: + 44 1904 544 666

Barclaycard
01604 230 230

Capital One
In the UK: 0800 952 5267
From abroad: + 44 115 993 8002

Citibank
In the UK: 0800 00 55 00
From abroad: + 44 207 500 55 00

Clydesdale Bank
0845 606 0622

The Co-operative Bank
In the UK: 0845 600 6000
From abroad: + 44 1695 53760

Diners Club
In the UK: 0870 1900 011
From abroad: + 44 1 252 513 500

Egg
In the UK: 08451 233 233
From abroad: + 44 1332 395 919

First Active
In the UK: 0870 600 0459
From abroad: + 44 131 549 8186

First Direct
In the UK: 08456 100 100
From abroad: + 44 113 234 5678

Goldfish
In the UK: 0800 281 881
From abroad: + 44 126 856 7402

Halifax
In the UK: 08457 20 30 99
From abroad: + 44 11 33 809 574

HSBC
In the UK: 08456 007 010
From abroad: + 44 1442 422 929

Lloyds TSB
In the UK: 0800 096 9779
From abroad: + 44 1702 278 270

Marks & Spencer
In the UK: 0845 900 0900
From abroad: + 44 12 44 879 080

Mastercard
0800 96 4767

MBNA
In the UK: 0800 062 062
From abroad: + 44 1244 672 111

Morgan Stanley
In the UK: 0800 02 88 990
From abroad: + 44 123 672 5678

National Irish Bank
Ireland: 1850 700 221
From abroad: + 353 1638 5000

Nationwide
Credit cards:

In the UK: 08457 99 22 22
From abroad: + 44 1268 567 213

Other cards
In the UK: 08457 30 20 10
From abroad: + 44 1793 456 789

NatWest
In the UK: 0870 600 0459
From abroad: + 44 142 370 0545

Northern Bank
In the UK: 08705 168 654
From abroad: + 44 113 288 1403

Partnership Card (John Lewis/Waitrose)
In the UK: 0800 015 0914
From abroad: + 44 121 214 5732

Royal Bank of Scotland
Credit cards:
0126 829 8929
Bank cards:
In the UK: 0870 513 3550
From abroad: + 44 131 317 88 99

Smile
In the UK: 0845 600 6000
From abroad: + 44 161 477 1927

Thomas Cook
Traveller's cheques:
In the UK: 0800 622 101
From abroad: + 44 1733 318 950

Ulster Bank
In the UK: 0870 600 0459
From abroad: + 44 131 549 81 86

Visa
0800 89 17 25

Woolwich
Open plan gold: 01604 230 230
Other open plan: 0845 0700 360
Other:
In the UK: 0845 677 0009
From abroad: + 44 12 55 225 335

Yorkshire Bank
In the UK: 08456 060 622
From abroad: + 44 113 288 1403

6

HEALTH

(For information about travel health insurance see the Insurance chapter.)

✳ IMMUNISATION ✳

For the latest information about which jabs you should have for travelling see the National Travel Health Network and Centre website www.nathnac.org.

YELLOW FEVER

Yellow fever, which can be fatal, is subject to an International Health Regulations (World Health Organisation) mandatory immunisation programme, which means you won't be able to enter certain countries unless you have an immunisation certificate.

COUNTRIES REQUIRING AN INTERNATIONAL HEALTH REGULATION IMMUNISATION CERTIFICATE

➢ Angola
➢ Benin
➢ Burkino Faso
➢ Cameroon
➢ Central African Republic
➢ Congo

> ➤ Democratic Republic of Congo
> ➤ Côte d'Ivoire
> ➤ El Salvador
> ➤ French Guiana
> ➤ Gabon
> ➤ Ghana
> ➤ Liberia
> ➤ Mali
> ➤ Niger
> ➤ Rwanda
> ➤ San Tome and Principe
> ➤ Sierra Leone
> ➤ Togo

NOTE: If you're travelling from a risk zone (see below) rather than direct from the UK many other countries may also require a certificate. For the latest details see www.who.int.

ADDITIONAL COUNTRIES THAT ARE RISK ZONES

> ➤ Bolivia
> ➤ Brazil
> ➤ Burundi
> ➤ Chad
> ➤ Colombia
> ➤ Ecuador
> ➤ Equatorial Guinea
> ➤ Ethiopia
> ➤ Gambia
> ➤ Guinea
> ➤ Guinea-Bissau
> ➤ Guyana
> ➤ Kenya
> ➤ Mauritania
> ➤ Nigeria
> ➤ Panama
> ➤ Peru
> ➤ Senegal
> ➤ Somalia
> ➤ Sudan
> ➤ Suriname
> ➤ Tanzania
> ➤ Trinidad and Tobago
> ➤ Uganda
> ➤ Venezuela

SYMPTOMS OF YELLOW FEVER

➤ Three to six day incubation period

➤ Fever, muscle pain (including noticeable back pain), shivering, loss of appetite, vomiting

➤ Around 85% of victims recover with no ill-effects after three or four days. The other 15% move into the toxic phase with jaundice and internal bleeding; around half of those die.

WHERE CAN I GET A JAB?

➤ See www.who.int.

Expert's tip ✛

Unlike the malarial mosquito, the variety that transmits yellow fever generally bites during the day so use an insect repellent at all times and keep skin covered when in high-risk areas.

MALARIA

Malaria is endemic in over 100 countries and can be caused by one of four different parasites, all of which are transmitted by mosquitoes. UK citizens are particularly vulnerable as they have no natural immunity.

COUNTRIES IN WHICH ALL FOUR TYPES OF MALARIA ARE FOUND

➤ Afghanistan
➤ Angola
➤ Bangladesh
➤ Belize
➤ Benin
➤ Bhutan
➤ Bolivia
➤ Bortswana
➤ Brazil
➤ Burkina Faso
➤ Burundi
➤ Cambodia
➤ Cameroon
➤ Cape Verde

- Central African Republic
- China
- Comoros
- Democratic Republic of Congo
- Côte D'Ivoire
- Dominican Republic
- Egypt
- Equatorial Guinea
- Ethiopia
- Gabon
- Ghana
- Guinea
- Guyana
- Honduras
- Indonesia
- Kenya
- Liberia
- Malawi
- Mali
- Mayotte
- Mozambique
- Namibia
- Nicaragua
- Nigeria
- Pakistan
- Papua New Guinea
- Philippines
- Sao Tome and Principe
- Senegal
- Solomon Islands
- South Africa
- Sudan
- Swaziland
- Chad
- Colombia
- Congo
- Costa Rica
- Dijbouti
- Ecuador
- El Salvador
- Eritrea
- French Guiana
- Gambia
- Guatemala
- Guinea-Bissau
- Haiti
- India
- Iran
- Lao
- Madagascar
- Malaysia
- Mauritania
- Mexico
- Myanmar
- Nepal
- Niger
- Oman
- Panama
- Peru
- Rwanda
- Saudia Arabia
- Sierre Leone
- Somalia
- Sri Lanka
- Suriname
- Tajikistan

- Tanzania
- Timore-Leste
- Uganda
- Venezuela
- Yemen
- Zimbabwe

- Thailand
- Togo
- Vanuatu
- Vietnam
- Zambia

COUNTRIES IN WHICH ONLY THE LESS SERIOUS P.VIVAX STRAIN IS FOUND

- Algeria
- Armenia
- Georgia
- Democratic People's Republic of Korea
- Kyrgyzstan
- Morocco
- Syria
- Turkmenistan

- Argentina
- Azerbaijan
- Iraq
- Republic of Korea
- Mauritius
- Paraguay
- Turkey
- Uzbekistan

SYMPTOMS OF MALARIA

- Fever with an incubation of seven days or longer. Four different species of parasite cause malaria: *plasmodium falciparum, p. vivax, p. ovale and p. malariae. P.* falciparum is the most dangerous and may be fatal if treatment is delayed more than 24 hours after the onset of fever.

WHERE CAN I GET PROTECTION?

To allow for possible side-effects to become apparent before you travel, you should contact your doctor at least six weeks prior to departure. Protection has become a complex business, due to drug resistance, and your GP may recommend you to a specialist in immunisation such as MASTA www.masta-travel-health.com.

There are now five different drugs and the one you require (or possibly two in combination) will depend on exactly where you are going. For full details see www.traveldoctor.co.uk.

Be sure to tell the doctor of any medical conditions you have and about any medicines you are taking so as to avoid any reaction with the anti-malarial drugs.

THE ABCD OF MALARIA PROTECTION

➤ Be **Aware** of the risk, the incubation period and the main symptoms.

➤ Avoid being **Bitten**.

➤ **Comply** with the drug regimen before, during and after travel, as appropriate, to prevent infection developing into a clinical disease

➤ Immediately seek **Diagnosis** and treatment if a fever develops one week up to three months after departure from a risk zone.

Expert's tip ✦

Malarial mosquitoes usually bite at night and are especially active at dusk and dawn, so keep skin covered then. Spray clothing and areas of skin that have to be bare with insect repellent. Sleep under mosquito netting impregnated with insecticide. It's also a good idea to spray the room, burn pyrethroid coils or use an insecticide that plugs into the mains.

Rule of thumb ☼

A serious fever developing less than one week after possible exposure is not malaria.

PROTECTION AGAINST OTHER DISEASES

Depending on where you're travelling you might require protection against:

➤ Diphtheria
➤ Hepatitis A
➤ Hepatitis B
➤ Japanese B encephalitis
➤ Meningitis
➤ Poliomyelitis
➤ Rabies
➤ Tetanus
➤ Tuberculosis
➤ Typhoid

Note that there is as yet no generally available vaccine against:

➤ Dengue fever – risk areas include Brazil and all the northern part of South America; much of Africa, especially Angola and Nigeria; India, Indonesia, Taiwan and Singapore. The disease is spread by a mosquito so take the same precautions as for malaria, but be aware that this mosquito bites *during the day* and is prevalent in *urban areas*.

For full details of health problems in different parts of the world and for a list of specialist clinics in your area see www.travel doctor.co.uk.

UNUSUAL OR
✳ ENVIRONMENTALLY-RELATED ✳
HEALTH HAZARDS

ALTITUDE

You don't have to be climbing Mount Everest to get high-altitude illness (HAI). It occurs when your body hasn't accustomed itself to less oxygen and can occur from 2100 metres, becoming common above 2700 metres. Mild effects include headache, nausea, insomnia and fatigue. Very occasionally Acute Mountain Sickness

(AMS) develops, leading to high-altitude pulmonary oedema or high-altitude cerebral oedema.

If you're suffering from any of the following don't travel to high altitudes:

➤ Unstable angina
➤ Pulmonary hypertension
➤ Severe chronic obstructive pulmonary disease
➤ Sickle-cell disease

WHEN TO SEEK MEDICAL ATTENTION

Consult a doctor if you suffer:

➤ Symptoms of AMS (headache, loss of appetite, nausea, insomnia, breathlessness or severe fatigue)

➤ Progressive shortness of breath with a cough

➤ Memory loss, confusion or an altered mental state

If possible descend immediately to a lower altitude.

Expert's tip ✛

♦ Avoid ascending directly to more than 2750 metres for an overnight stay – ascend gradually and break the journey for at least one night at 2000-2500 metres to help prevent AMS. If it's unavoidable, ask your doctor or travel clinic about drug treatments such as acetazolamide.
♦ Avoid over-exertion and alcohol for the first 24 hours at altitude and drink extra water.

HEAT EXHAUSTION AND HEAT STROKE

Overheating comes in two stages:

➤ Heat exhaustion – easily remedied by getting somewhere cool, resting and sipping water or, better still, a sports drink with electrolytes.

➤ Heat stroke – far more serious and potentially fatal because it means the body's cooling system has broken down. Victims need to be cooled with wet cloths or even immersion in water. Get help as soon as possible.

Rule of thumb ☼

In heat exhaustion the skin feels cold and sweaty but in heat stroke the skin is dry, pink and warm.

Expert's tip ✦

♦ Drink more than usual in hot weather (preferably something containing electrolytes, such as a sports drink) and add salt to food.

♦ Older people and children are particularly vulnerable.

♦ Where possible take a daily shower and wear loose cotton clothing.

SUNBURN

The ultraviolet rays from the sun can damage not only your skin but also your eyes, so both should be protected. The intensity of UV radiation is measured by the *Global Solar UV Index* which increasingly appears on weather reports and forecasts (see Weather).

➤ Never let your skin get burnt – if you want a tan build it up *very gradually*.

➤ Adults *and children* should wear sunglasses when the UV Index is 3 or higher.

➤ Keep out of the sun from mid-morning to mid-afternoon if the UV Index is 6 or more.

➤ Bald men should wear a hat if the UV Index is 3 or higher; everyone should wear a hat if the UV Index is 6 or higher.

Examine your skin once a month; report anything suspicious, especially changes to moles, to your doctor.

THE SUNSCREEN CONTROVERSY

While it's widely accepted that sunscreens help prevent burning, *many scientists believe they actually increase the risk of the dangerous skin cancer known as malignant melanoma.*

Let's look first at what that Sun Protection Factor (SPF) actually means:

SPF	Proportion of UVA blocked
10	90%
20	95%
30	96.66%
60	98.33%

In theory, the SPF can be used as a multiplier. In other words, if you could normally remain in the sun for 10 minutes without burning then a sunscreen of SPF 10 would allow you to stay for 100 minutes and an SPF 60 would allow you to stay for 10 hours. However, the real picture is complicated.

In the first place, there is another kind of dangerous ultraviolet radiation, known as UVB, against which sunscreens are far less effective. Secondly, some scientists say that only 8% of melanomas are caused by sunburn and that the remainder are caused by other DNA damage *potentially including that from chemicals in sunscreen.*

Expert's tip ✛

The safest course is that you avoid sunscreens and only remain in the sun for the amount of time you naturally can without burning — only use sunscreen when exposure is unavoidable (for example, when skiing).

DEEP VEIN THROMBOSIS

Deep vein thrombosis is a clotting of the blood in any of the deep veins of the body, but most often in the calf. It can be caused by long periods of immobility, such as on a long-haul flight. One of the first symptoms is severe pain in the affected part. Medical treatment should be sought immediately because the situation can become life threatening if part of the clot breaks off.

WHO IS AT RISK?

The following factors increase the risk:

➤ Heart problems
➤ Dehydration
➤ Severe infections
➤ Being over the age of 60
➤ Pregnancy or within the two months after childbirth
➤ Recent surgery
➤ Cancer or the treatment of cancer
➤ Certain blood conditions
➤ A personal or family experience of DVT
➤ Obesity
➤ Illness
➤ Hormone problems and the oral contraceptive
➤ Varicose veins
➤ Inflammatory bowel disease

SICKNESS AND DIARRHOEA

These are two of the commonest travellers' ailments and usually caused by contaminated food and water.

Avoid:

➤ Obviously contaminated food (flies, visible dirt, anything that smells 'off').

➤ Any food which has been standing for any length of time and is lukewarm.

➤ Anything which could have been contaminated by chemicals.

➤ In developing countries: raw meat, fish, shellfish or eggs; raw fruit and vegetables unless you peel them; salads and anything that may have been 'washed' in contaminated water; ice-cream from open containers; any drink from an already opened bottle; ice; tap water.

➤ Tap water (brush your teeth with bottled water from a safe source and keep your mouth closed when showering).

HOW TO MAKE WATER SAFE

STEP 1. Filter cloudy and dirty looking water through a cloth or, better still, using a portable filter bought from a specialist travel or hiking shop.

STEP 2. Either boil the clear water for several minutes or treat it with iodine.

Expert's tip ✦
Ultraviolet light will kill viruses and bacteria. You can now buy a portable, battery-operated device to immerse in a cup of clear water. It will purify about half a litre in a minute.

HOW TO TREAT TRAVELLER'S DIARRHOEA:

➤ Rule Number One – do not become dehydrated. It is particularly important to be vigilant with children and the elderly.

➤ If the problem persists for more than 24 hours take Oral Rehydration Salts. If you don't have shop-bought ORS then an alternative is six level teaspoons of sugar and one level tea-spoon of salt in one litre of safe drinking water.

➤ If the condition persists more than three days medical help should be sought.

➤ If you feel you can eat, try boiled rice, bananas, clear soups and crisps.

Expert's tip ✦

If you're taking the oral contraceptive pill absorption may be affected by sickness and diarrhoea. Keep taking the pill but use back-up methods of contraception as well until you begin a new cycle.

JET LAG

According to NASA, you need one day for every one-hour time zone you cross. In other words, if you cross five times zones you'll need five days to adjust properly.

Expert's tip ✦

♦ Set your watch at the destination time as soon as you're settled into your aircraft seat.

♦ Consider that to be the time; never again think of the time in the place you're leaving.

♦ Only sleep during the flight if it's night-time in your destination.

♦ Once at your destination, live in accordance with local time; don't sleep or nap during the day.

♦ Your circadian rhythms are regulated by light, so do your best to fully experience natural daylight in your destination by getting outdoors as much as possible.

TRAVEL SICKNESS

If it moves and you're travelling in it (from a Ferris wheel to Ferrari) you can experience travel sickness. Some people, especially children, are far more prone than others.

Travel sickness can be caused by:

➤ Movement – sudden repeated changes in direction or velocity.

➤ Visual effects – when the eyes can't take in what's happening to the body (even some films can make you feel travel sick).

➤ Eye strain – if you're repeatedly having to refocus your eyes, such as when trying to read in a car.

➤ Nervous system confusion – the balance system of the inner ear, skin, eyes and muscles can all send out different signals.

TREATMENTS THAT MAY HELP

➤ Travel sickness pills taken at least two hours before. (Warning: they may cause drowsiness.)

➤ Acupressure – elasticised bands that apply pressure to a recognised acupuncture spot about one inch up the arm from the wrist are widely available.

➤ Ginger – chew slowly on a piece of root.

➤ Fernet Branca or Angostura Bitters, diluted in water, or Coca-Cola help some people.

Expert's tip ✦

♦ Sit as close as possible to the centre of motion where the movement is least. On a boat that will be in the middle, close to the waterline; on an aircraft it's usually the seats aligned with the forward part of the wings.

♦ In a car or coach sit as close to the front as possible.

- ◆ *Focus your eyes on a distant point, usually the horizon.*
- ◆ *Relax.*
- ◆ *Get plenty of fresh air.*
- ◆ *Avoid strong smells.*
- ◆ *Avoid other ill passengers.*
- ◆ *For severe sea sickness lie face down in the dark fore and aft (that is, not across the boat).*

BITES

INSECTS

Biting insects are irritating and can be dangerous (see Yellow Fever and Malaria above).

Cover up bare skin as much as possible; wear light-coloured clothing so insects are more visible.

Use an insect repellent containing DEET, applied every two to three hours.

➢ Sleep under a mosquito net with mesh no larger than 1.5 mm and treated with insect repellent.

➢ Burn mosquito coils or use an insecticide that plugs into the mains.

➢ If you have air conditioning, use it and close the windows.

➢ In tick-infested areas examine yourself several times a day – the more quickly a tick is removed the less likely it is to transmit infection.

Expert's tip ✦

♦ Don't forget to apply insect repellent to your clothing as well. This lasts longer than on skin and will give an additional level of protection. Insect repellent should not be used on sunburned or broken skin.

♦ Ticks that have attached themselves can be encouraged to let go by dabbing them with alcohol or touching them with the head of a match just blown out; if that doesn't work they can be pulled off with tweezers or, if nothing else is available, gripped between fingernails – be sure to take hold of the head not the body.

DOGS AND OTHER ANIMALS

Dogs and some other animals can transmit rabies. Normally vaccination is only counselled if you are travelling to a high-risk zone and are going to be more than 24 hours from adequate medical help. All animal bites should be treated as serious and the following steps should be taken:

➢ Capture the animal if practical, so it can be tested.

➢ Wash the wound for at least five minutes under running water.

➢ Treat with an iodine preparation or surgical spirit (alcohol).

➢ Seek medical help immediately.

➢ On return from your trip contact your own doctor.

Expert's tip ✦

Don't attempt to pat or play with animals you don't know to be safe, however cuddly or appealing they may look.

SNAKES

There are some 2,900 species of snakes worldwide of which

around a quarter are considered venomous but only some 250 are able to kill a person with one bite. What's more, even when a venomous snake does bite it may not inject venom. Statistically you're very unlikely to be bitten by any snake and if you follow the *Expert's tips* below the chance will be infinitesimally small.

If you should be bitten by a snake:

➢ Don't wash the bite (any venom on the skin can be used to identify the correct antivenin).

➢ Do not cut the bitten area or attempt to suck the venom out.

➢ Do not try to catch the snake.

➢ If in a suitable place, bandage the wound firmly (an elastic bandage is ideal) and then continue bandaging away from the heart then back towards the heart. Do not cut off the blood flow – the aim, instead, is to restrict the movement of the venom in the lymphatic vessels which is the route by which most snake venoms spread. In difficult parts of the body try to find some other means of applying pressure.

➢ If bitten on a limb it should be immobilised with a splint.

➢ Move as little as possible.

➢ Get medical help.

Rule of thumb ☼

The fact that you've been bitten by a snake doesn't mean that any venom has been injected. You'll know it has been if you experience:
- *Discharge of blood from the wound*
- *Swelling and severe pain at the site of the wound*
- *Diarrhoea*

- *Convulsions*
- *Blurred vision, dizziness, fainting*

Expert's tip ✦

♦ Never try to handle a snake – most bites happen this way.
♦ Never walk barefoot or with open sandals in risky areas.
♦ Never sit down on or put hands or feet under rocks or pieces of wood without first carefully investigating.
♦ Make sure you have a torch with you for walking at night.
♦ Always thoroughly and carefully check boots, shoes and beds for unwanted visitors.

OTHER STINGING AND BITING CREATURES

Some **scorpions** are dangerous to humans (for example, in Mexico, New Mexico and Arizona) but most are not. They are nocturnal and you are, therefore, unlikely to encounter them unless you disturb their hiding places, such as crevices in rocks or, possibly, cupboards – always examine your room, bed, clothes, shoes and so on in areas where scorpions are known to be a problem.

Spiders are more readily encountered since they hunt in the daytime. Most dangerous are the Australian Sydney funnel-web spider, the North American brown recluse, the South American banana spider, the 'widow' group and – for people with allergies – the tarantula, mostly found in South America.

Treatment

➢ Treat scorpion stings and spider bites the same as snake bites (but capture the spider for identification if you can).

➢ Ice on the bite or sting may reduce the pain.

➢ Get medical help as quickly as possible.

➢ The doctor may give a pain-killing injection.

➢ There are antiserums for some scorpion and spider venoms.

UNUSUAL DISEASES

➢ Chikungunya (viral infection spread by mosquitoes)

➢ Cholera (bacterial infection causing severe diarrhoea)

➢ Dengue Fever (mosquito-borne disease affecting around 50 million people a year)

➢ Ebola (a highly contagious virus)

➢ Lassa Fever (viral disease mostly in West Africa and spread by rats)

➢ Leishmaniasis (spread by sandflies and even exists in the Mediterranean)

➢ Lyme disease (spread by ticks and existing in the UK as well as further afield)

➢ River blindess (spread by blackflies)

➢ SARS (a new virus which spread globally in 2003)

➢ Schistomiasis – also known as Bilharziasis (spread through contaminated water via the skin)

➢ Tularaemia (bacterial infection spread to humans from animals)

➢ West Nile Virus (usually spread by mosquitoes)

➢ For further information on these diseases see www.travel health.co.uk/diseases/index.html or www.who.int or contact

the Hospital for Tropical Diseases 020 795 07799 or the
Liverpool School of Tropical Medicine 0906 7010095.

➤ For country by country reports on disease risks see
www.fco.gov.uk/travel.

➤ For general health advice for travellers see:
www.dh.gov.uk/PolicyandGuidance/HealthAdviceforTravellers/
fs/en.

SEXUALLY TRANSMITTED DISEASES

Condoms are recommended during the first six months of any
relationship, so if you have sex with someone you meet while
travelling they should always be used. Nevertheless, the effective-
ness of condoms varies according to the disease:

➤ HIV – highly effective

➤ Gonorrhea and chlamydia – quite effective

➤ Herpes, syphilis and HPV – quite effective but only if the
affected area is covered by the condom.

FIRST AID KITS

A first aid kit is always a good idea. Its contents will depend on
where you're going, what you plan to do and your own health
situation. For that reason it's usually best to make up your own kit
but you can buy them pre-packed.

Contents should include:

➤ Sticking plasters
➤ Gauze pads, a roll of gauze and adhesive tape
➤ Moleskin (if you're planning a lot of walking)
➤ Various bandages
➤ Antiseptic

➤ Tweezers
➤ Scissors
➤ Painkillers
➤ Antacid tablets
➤ Antihistamines in case of allergic reactions
➤ Treatment for holiday diarrhoea
➤ Personal medicines
➤ For certain areas consider taking advanced medical supplies such as sealed syringes and needles, suture equipment and antiseptic wipes. These are not for you to use but to be handed in to any hospital or clinic where hygiene or equipment cannot be guaranteed

Expert's tip ✦

♦ Keep vital medicines in your hand luggage.
♦ Some countries limit the amount of certain drugs which can be carried in and out. If they're critical to you check with the embassy.
♦ Keep things in original packaging for identification, dosage and protection.

7

INSURANCE

If you don't have travel insurance it's not just you but also your bank balance that could get very sick.

Expert's tip

If you're allergic to any drugs or are on any particular medication, keep a type-written note with your passport or medical card, in translation if possible. If it's a matter of life or death wear a medical bracelet to alert medical staff should you be unconscious. Put 'medical bracelet UK' into your search engine or see:

♦ *www.medicaltags.co.uk*
♦ *www.medical-bracelets.co.uk*
♦ *www.patient.co.uk*

✴ TRAVEL HEALTH INSURANCE ✴

The European Health Insurance Card (EHIC) has replaced the E111. It entitles the holder to free or discounted medical treatment throughout the European Economic Area (EEA) as well as in Switzerland. The EEA comprises the EU countries plus Iceland, Liechtenstein and Norway. The EHIC is normally valid for three to five years and covers state-provided medical treatment for accident or illness, on the same basis as an insured person living in that country. You can apply for a card:

➤ Online at www.ehic.org.uk/Internet/home.do

➤ By collecting a form at the Post Office

➤ By telephoning 0845 606 2030

However, there are still things that won't be covered by your EHIC (such as recovery from a mountain after a skiing accident or repatriation to the UK by air ambulance) so it's prudent to get additional insurance for the EHIC area (and strongly recommended outside).

As a UK citizen you'll also be entitled to limited free health treatment in certain other countries:

➤ Anguilla (minor emergency treatment)

➤ Australia (public hospital treatment)

➤ Barbados (hospital treatment, treatment at polyclinics, ambulance travel, prescribed medicines for children and the elderly)

➤ Bosnia and Herzegovina (hospital treatment, some GP-type medical treatment, some dental treatment)

➤ British Virgin Islands (hospital and other medical treatment for the over 70s and children)

➤ Bulgaria (public medical, dental and hospital treatment)

➤ Channel Islands (Guernsey/Alderney – hospital in-patient treatment; Jersey – hospital in-patient and out-patient treatment plus ambulance travel)

➤ Croatia (hospital treatment, some dental treatment, some other medical treatment)

➤ Falkland Islands (hospital treatment, dental treatment, other medical treatment, prescribed medicines, ambulance travel)

➤ Gibraltar (GP and dental treatment at the Primary Care Medical Centres; public hospital in-patient treatment)

➤ Macedonia (hospital treatment, some dental treatment, general GP-type treatment)

➤ Montserrat (treatment at government medical institutions for over 65s and under16s; dental treatment for children)

➤ New Zealand (dental treatment for under16s, public hospital in-patient treatment)

➤ Romania (hospital treatment, some GP-type treatment and some dental treatment)

➤ Russia (treatment in state hospitals)

➤ St Helena (hospital out-patient clinics)

➤ Serbia and Montenegro (hospital treatment, GP-type treatment, some dental treatment)

➤ Turks and Caicos Islands (all medical treatment for over 65s and under 16s; Grand Turk Island – dental clinic treatment, prescribed medicines, ambulance travel; Outer Islands – medical treatment at government clinics; prescribed medicines)

➤ Former USSR – Armenia, Azerbaijan, Georgia, Kazakhstan, Kyrgyzstan, Moldova, Tajikistan, Turkmenistan, Uzbekistan, Ukraine – (hospital and some GP-type treatment, some dental treatment)

OLDER TRAVELLERS

Older travellers can find it difficult to obtain travel health insurance just when they need it the most. Try:

www.ageconcern.org.uk 0845 600 3348 or visit your local Age
Concern

www.saga.co.uk 0800 015 8055

> *Expert's tip* ✚
>
> Take adequate supplies of regular medicines with you and a note of the
> generic names in case they are lost.

GENERAL TRAVEL INSURANCE

Of course, there's a lot more to travel insurance than health.
When travelling you tend to have quite a lot of valuables with you,
you're in places you don't know, and you'll probably be doing
things you never do at home (such as horse riding, skiing, diving
and so on).

There's a huge choice of policies and prices which you can
compare at:

➤ www.moneysupermarket.com

➤ www.moneysavingexpert.com/insurance/cheap-travel-
   insurance

Look out for the following points:

➤ Are pre-existing medical conditions covered? You'll inevitably
   have to confess all before you buy the policy and you may see
   premiums go up. But if you're not frank the insurance could
   be invalid.

➤ Are extreme sports covered? Things like diving and skiing
   usually require special cover – and skiing off-piste may require
   still extra cover.

➤ Note the maximum age limit on the policy. These vary wildly from company to company (from as young as 39 in some cases).

➤ Does the policy cover repatriation by air in medical emergencies?

➤ What is the medical costs maximum? Look for at least £1 million but in North America think more of £2 million.

➤ Pregnant? Then you must inform your insurer and take out special cover.

➤ Is there a policy excess? That is, do you have to pay the first part of any loss?

➤ On what grounds can you recover your costs if you have to cancel your trip?

➤ How long do you have to be delayed before you're entitled to compensation?

Rule of thumb ☼

- *If you go away twice a year (including weekend breaks) an annual policy will probably be cheaper than two single-trip policies.*
- *If you're going to the USA even just once an annual policy could be cheaper than a single-trip policy.*

Expert's tip ✦

When you pay for travel with a credit card you'll usually get insurance cover for accidents but other kinds of cover may not be included. Check the details and, if appropriate, get extra insurance.

8

LANGUAGE PROBLEMS

You're in a foreign country, you don't speak the language and you need to enquire about a rail ticket. What do you do? One solution is to take out your mobile, phone a telephone translation service, explain what you want to say, then hand the phone to the ticket clerk. Simple! And it needn't cost very much.

To find a telephone translation service, put the name of the foreign language into your search engine together with the words 'telephone translation' and see what comes up. Some services are orientated towards tourists and brief conversations. Others are orientated towards businessmen and long negotiations. And if you'll be using specialist jargon (in the medical or electronics fields, for example) you'll need to find a service that can cope. Compare several before deciding – prices can vary considerably.

Expert's tip +

♦ Mobile or portable phones handed back and forth work best.

♦ If you use a loudspeaking telephone be sure there are no extraneous noises (rustling papers, outside traffic and so on).

♦ Speak to the interpreter just as if you were speaking to the person (don't prefix with confusing phrases such as "I'd like to tell her that . . .)

SOME TELEPHONE TRANSLATION SERVICES:

➤ www.inrealtimetranslation.com 0845 838 1051

➤ www.kwintessential.co.uk 0845 124 9615

➤ www.london-translations.co.uk 0207 021 0888 Operates
 24/7 covering 150 languages

➤ www.thebigword.com 0870 748 8044

➤ www.chinaonecall.com 0845 500 2122 Operates 24/7
 Specialist in Mandarin/English.

Rule of thumb ☼

*When you're speaking English to someone with little or no
English:*
➤ *Use signs and plenty of facial expressions*
➤ *Speak slowly but not loudly*
➤ *Repeat your meaning using different vocabulary each time —
 with luck you'll hit on a word that's similar to one in the
 language of the person you're speaking to.*

When you're trying to speak a foreign language you barely know:
➤ *Use signs and plenty of facial expressions*
➤ *Speak slowly but not loudly*
➤ *Precede each sentence with a simple well-known phrase so
 that the person you're speaking to can 'tune in' to your
 accent. For example, in French, you could simply begin with
 "S'il vous plaît" (Please) or in Spanish you might try "Puede
 usted enseñarme?" (Can you show me?).*

9

MINIMISING YOUR ENVIRONMENTAL IMPACT

Travel can be bad for the planet. The reason is simple. Transport burns energy, energy mostly comes from fossil fuels, fossil fuels release carbon dioxide, and more carbon dioxide in the atmosphere means more global warming.

So how can you minimise your impact? In descending order of fuel efficiency your options are:

➤ Walking
➤ Cycling
➤ Fuel-efficient car with all seats taken
➤ Coach
➤ Train
➤ Fuel-efficient car with average number of passengers (1.56)
➤ Fuel-efficient car with driver only
➤ Flying/gas-guzzling car with driver only
➤ Cruising

Always aim to use the most fuel-efficient transport.

✳ IS THERE REALLY GLOBAL ✳ WARMING?

Yes, really. And a good thing, too. Otherwise the planet would be uninhabitable. The fact is the greenhouse effect has existed for eons and without it the average temperature of the planet would now be −18°C. In other words, about 33°C lower than it is now. We wouldn't be writing this and you wouldn't be reading it, if it wasn't for the greenhouse effect. None of us would exist.

The greenhouse effect works like this. The main constituents of the atmosphere are transparent to heat radiation. They are:

➤ Nitrogen
➤ Oxygen

If they were the only gases in the atmosphere, the heat generated on Earth by the sun would be radiated back into space. But, fortunately, there are additional gases present in small quantities which can trap some of the heat. The principal ones are:

➤ Water vapour
➤ Carbon dioxide
➤ Methane

You've probably noticed the effect for yourself. When the sky is clear the night-time temperature falls more than when it's cloudy. That's because the clouds – water vapour – are exerting their greenhouse effect.

All this has happened naturally – that is to say, without any man-made intervention – which is why scientists call it the *natural greenhouse effect*. What's happening now is that we're all adding to that greenhouse effect by burning fossil fuels to power our cars and heat our homes. You can see the effect of that in the table overleaf.

THE FIVE WARMEST YEARS WORLDWIDE SINCE THE 1890s

1   2005
2   1998
3   2002
4   2003
5   2004   *Source: NASA*

✳ HOW BAD COULD IT GET? ✳

The range of mainstream predictions at the moment is that temperatures will increase by between 1.4°C and 5.8°C over the next hundred years – that's roughly two to 10 times more than in the past hundred years.

✳ IS IT ALL DUE TO CARBON ✳ DIOXIDE?

This is how the concentration of carbon dioxide has altered in the Earth's atmosphere:

➤ Pre-industrial concentration – 280 ppm (parts per million)

➤ Present concentration – 380 ppm.

Those who dispute human influence on global warming have got to explain why carbon dioxide *does* warm the planet at concentrations up to 280 ppm but exerts no further warming effect at higher concentrations. That's a difficult trick to pull off. It would be the same as trying to argue that one centimetre of insulation in your home keeps the temperature up but two centimetres doesn't make any difference. It's just not logical.

But, yes, there are other gases that trap heat. Here are the main ones, compared with carbon dioxide:

	Lifetime in the atmosphere	Pre-industrial concentration	Concentration in 1998
Carbon dioxide	5 – 200 yrs	280 ppm	365 ppm
Methane	12 yrs	700 ppb	1,745 ppb
Nitrous oxide	114 yrs	270 ppb	314 ppb
Chlorofuorocarbon-11	45 yrs	0	268 ppt
Hydrofluorcarbon-23	260 yrs	0	14 ppt
Perfluoromethane	50,000 yrs	40 ppt	80 ppt

Ppm = parts per million; ppb = parts per billion; ppt = parts per trillion.

As you can see, carbon dioxide is the most abundant greenhouse gas but it's not, in fact, the most powerful. If its *global warming potential* is given a value of one, then, over a 20-year period, methane is 62 times stronger and over the course of a century nitrous oxide is almost 300 times more powerful. However, because of its abundance, carbon dioxide is the single largest contributor to what scientists call *radiative forcing* – the process by which human activities intensify the natural greenhouse effect.

The most frightening figures are those in the first column. Even if all man-made emissions are stopped now – which would be impossible – the planet would still heat up because it takes years, and even centuries, for these gases to disappear from the air.

YOUR TRAVEL POLLUTION CALCULATOR

Here's a calculator to tell you roughly how much pollution any journey will create. It's necessarily only a broad picture because your personal total will depend very much on variables such as the load factor of the plane, coach, train or car that you're travelling in and the route taken.

Nevertheless, the general message is pretty clear – go by coach, train or sailing ship whenever possible. If you want to go by car make sure (a) its fuel consumption is among the lowest possible, and (b) every seat is taken. Although a full medium-sized car produces less pollution per mile than a plane, don't forget that a car usually has to travel a greater distance to get to the same destination. And if there's only you in a large car then it's by far the most polluting form of land transport. Avoid flying and cruising.

Destination (capital city)	Carbon Dioxide emissions for a one-way journey from London by:					
	Air	Car	Train	Coach	Cruise	Sailing
Belgium/France	160	55	45	30	–	–
Ireland	240	80	65	45	–	–
Switzerland	380	80	90	60		
Germany	465	155	110	75		
Austria/Spain	625	210	150	100		
Italy/Poland	740	250	175	120		
Tunisia	925	310	250	180	1800	200
Greece	1200	400	290	200	2500	250
Egypt	1500	665	500	400	3000	300
UAE	2100	835	650	500	4000	400
USA/Canada	2300	–	–	–	3000	300
India	2600	900	850	550	5000	525
Jamaica	3000	–	–	–	4000	425
Mexico	3500	–	–	–	4500	475
Thailand/Sth Africa	3700	1250	1150	800	4000/ 7000	450/ 750
Australia	5400	2000	2000	1300	11000	1000

(Units: Kg of CO_2 per passenger)

NOTES:

(1) *Cars.* The figures are based on the average number of passengers in a medium-sized car which is 1.56. Of course, it's impossible to have 1.56 people in a car, but you get the broad idea. Obviously if there are three of you in the car you can more or less halve the figure. And if you have four people in a low-consumption car such as a Toyota Prius you can halve it again.

(2) *Boats.* It has to be kept in mind that while planes fly fairly directly to their destinations other forms of transport have to take more convoluted and therefore longer routes. A cruise ship sailing from the UK to Greece, for example, will cover almost double the straight-line distance. The figures for sailing ships are somewhat notional since we don't know the size of the boat, how many people are aboard nor how often it will be necessary to run the engine when the wind is insufficient.

But they give you an idea of the scale of difference between a cruise ship and a sailing boat.

(3) *General.* These figures should only be treated as a rough guide, as there are so many variables. In many cases it isn't very practical to take, say, the train rather than the plane. And some overland routes would, of course, require one or more legs to be done by ferry, thus increasing the total amount of pollution.

➤ If you'd like to know more about travel and the environment see *The Green Travel Guide*, also published by White Ladder Press.

THINGS YOU CAN DO TO REDUCE YOUR TRAVEL IMPACT

➤ Use the least-polluting form of transport whenever you can.

➤ Don't use jetskis, quad bikes or trail bikes. They create noise, pollution, nuisance and danger for other people.

MONEY

They say money talks. Yes, it says 'goodbye'. And never more quickly than when travelling. So for that reason, as well as security and versatility, it's best not to rely on any one source.

✳ HOW TO TAKE MONEY ABROAD ✳

It's a good idea to have a mixture of:

➤ Cash
➤ Credit and debit cards
➤ Traveller's cheques

CASH

You don't want to arrive without at least enough foreign currency to pay for a coffee or a taxi or deal with one of life's minor emergencies. If you're out of luck you may not find anywhere to change money and be in difficulties. So be sure to have some foreign currency in your pocket or purse before you get there.

It's worth shopping around for the best deal, especially if you're changing a large amount. Bear in mind the currency you want may not be in stock so do this in good time. Be sure to compare like with like. There can be as many as four different costs involved in buying foreign currency:

➤ The exchange rate

➤ The commission

➤ The handling charge

➤ The delivery charge (if you're having the currency delivered to you)

So don't just ask what the exchange rate is. Be sure to find out the total cost. And ask if you can exchange unused currency free at the end of your holiday. That can be a worthwhile perk. If so, be sure to keep your receipt as proof of the original transaction.

When you're at your destination, only exchange currency at a bank or bona fide exchange dealer. Otherwise you run the risk of forged notes – and in some countries you may be breaking the law. Keep your receipts.

FORGED NOTES

Counterfeit money is relatively common and tourists who aren't familiar with a currency can easily be victims. Fortunately there's a simple solution – the counterfeit detector pen. Very cheap, it leaves a permanent mark on forged notes but not on genuine notes, and works with about a hundred currencies including sterling and the euro: www.maplin.co.uk 0870 429 6000.

Expert's tip ✦

♦ Some banks and building societies offer commission-free currency.
♦ Some gold cards offer commission-free currency as a benefit.
♦ The post office offers major currencies commission-free.

Rule of thumb ☼
When buying foreign currency, you'll usually get the best rate in

the country whose currency you're paying in. In other words, when changing sterling into euros, you're most likely to get the best rate in the UK; when changing dollars into sterling you'll most likely get the best rate in the USA.

For security reasons, it obviously isn't a good idea to carry large amounts of cash. If, for some reason, you do need a lot, carry it in a money belt. If there are two of you, divide it up. If you should be unfortunate, report the theft to the police and ask for a copy of the statement for your insurance company.

Rule of thumb ✿

If you have travel insurance, check how much cash it covers and don't carry more than that.

Expert's tip ✦

♦ Don't keep your cash, plastic money and traveller's cheques in the same place, just in case they all get stolen. Divide them, and other valuables, between pockets, wallet/handbag and money belt (and between you, if you're a couple).

♦ Watch out for the 'slow count' – the shopkeeper counts out your change very slowly with exaggerated pauses hoping you'll become impatient and scoop up your money without checking it.

♦ And watch out for worthless coins in your change – they could be out-of-date or they could be lower-value coins of a different currency.

WARNING

Since 2007 you are required to declare cash sums of €10,000 or more (about £7,500) if travelling outside the EU, or if returning to the UK from a country outside the EU. Note that cash includes traveller's cheques (see below) and banker's drafts. Failure to do so could result in the money being confiscated.

✳ TRAVELLER'S CHEQUES ✳

Traveller's cheques are the safest method of taking money abroad because if they're stolen you won't be liable for a single penny. And, normally, they can be replaced within 24 hours (although you may have to wait longer in some destinations). However, they do have some possible drawbacks:

➤ In some countries (such as China) and in the more out-of-the-way spots it may be difficult to change traveller's cheques or spend them.

➤ In some destinations, changing traveller's cheques can take a long time.

➤ Traveller's cheques are expensive – there's a fee on issue and you'll pay again when you cash them.

Expert's tip ✦

♦ Enquire which brand of traveller's cheques is most widely accepted in your destination. Some prefer one, some prefer another.

♦ In case of theft, make two notes of the place you bought the traveller's cheques, the date you bought them and the serial numbers. Keep one note with you (not with the cheques) and leave the other with a reliable person back home.

CREDIT AND DEBIT CARDS

Plastic money is extremely convenient. Cards are small, light and widely accepted. Credit cards allow you to live now and pay later. And there may be bonuses such as purchase protection, discount travel insurance, air miles and even private airport lounges. However, they can be quite an expensive way of buying goods and services and they may be a *very* expensive way of drawing cash:

➤ Some credit card companies add a foreign loading of up to 2.75% to purchases as well as to cash withdrawals.

➤ The charge for withdrawing cash on a credit card may be up to 2% *plus* the foreign loading *plus* interest as a cash advance.

So check exactly what charges you'll have to pay and organise your payment methods accordingly.

If your card is stolen, report the theft immediately you know. You won't be liable for any fraudulent expenditure after that. Prior to the report you're usually liable for the first £50.

CREDIT CARD PROTECTION

Expert's tip ✦

♦ Compare card charges abroad at a site such as www.moneysuper
market.com and, if appropriate, apply for a cheaper card in addition to, or instead of, your existing card.

♦ Ask your bank or credit card company if they have any special reduced-charge arrangements with companies overseas.

♦ Unless you're a frequent traveller, notify your credit card company about your holiday dates and destinations before departure. Otherwise you may find your initial foreign transactions subject to extra security checks.

♦ Keep a record of your card numbers, bank account details and the emergency telephone numbers in a safe place quite separate from your plastic money.

♦ Always check your statement carefully to guard against 'skimming' – someone using your details to make purchases. You won't have to pay as long as you can prove it wasn't you.

♦ Take extra care in the following credit card fraud hot spots:
  – Turkey   – France
  – Spain   – United States

– Italy	– China
– Thailand	– Republic of Ireland
– India	– Netherlands

If you subscribe to a credit card protection scheme you can cancel all your cards with just one telephone call (see Emergencies for individual telephone numbers). But you should still contact the police as well. Some schemes include useful emergency help such as a cash advance, payment of hotel bills and payment for flights home.

Companies include:

➤ www.cpp.co.uk Card Protection Plan 01904 544 500
➤ www.pinnacle.co.uk Pinnacle Insurance plc 020 8207 9000
➤ www.st-andrews.co.uk St. Andrew's Membership Services
    0870 850 6 850

YOUR OWN CHEQUES IN AN EMERGENCY

In some of the most popular tourist areas abroad you may be able to cash a normal cheque at a bank provided it's supported by a valid cheque guarantee card. However, the commission rate is likely to be quite high. It's best to reserve this option for emergencies.

FOREIGN CURRENCY LEFT OVER

If you did your homework you may have found a company that not only offered a good initial deal but also to change left-over foreign currency for free. Even so, it's smart to choose the moment when the exchange rate is most advantageous (in other words, sterling is *weak* against the foreign currency). Or you could simply keep your foreign currency until next time, if you're going again soon.

Aim to have no foreign coins left at the end of your holiday – you may find it difficult to change them and the rate will be poor.

✳ AN OVERSEAS BANK ACCOUNT ✳

Expert's tip ✦

If you do have foreign coins left over, why not donate them to charity? There are collection boxes in some airports and charity shops.

You can only do so much with a UK credit card so if you intend to buy a holiday home abroad you'll need a bank account in that country. These are the kinds of things you might want it for:

➤ Helping prove your identity

➤ Getting a telephone line, water, electricity

➤ Paying local rates, services, builders.

In most cases yours will be an expatriate bank account and the tax rules will probably be different to those that apply to domestic customers.

Expert's tip ✦

Your bank abroad should be able to issue you with a debit card but probably not a credit card, since you won't have established a credit record in the country. However, if you'd like one it may be possible if you deposit funds in a secure account up to the credit limit you'd like.

OFFSHORE BANKING

It's perfectly legal to have a bank account in a third country – neither the UK nor where you have your holiday home. This is something you need to discuss with an accountant specialising in the subject.

PAYING IN ADVANCE

It's a good idea to pay for as many things as possible (hotels, car hire and so on) in advance of leaving the UK if:

➤ You think the British pound is going to weaken relative to the currency of the country or countries you plan to visit.

✳ THE EURO ZONE ✳

If you're travelling around in Europe you can now use euros in more than a score of countries, which could result in a significant saving in foreign exchange commissions.

Malta and Cyprus (excluding the Turkish Republic of Northern Cyprus, which is recognised only by Turkey) both joined the euro on 1 January 2008, bringing the Eurozone to a total of 15 countries. In fact, there are now more people living in 'Euroland' than in the USA. The countries are:

➤ Austria
➤ Belgium
➤ Cyprus
➤ Finland
➤ France
➤ Germany
➤ Greece
➤ Ireland
➤ Italy
➤ Luxembourg
➤ Malta
➤ Netherlands
➤ Portugal
➤ Slovenia
➤ Spain

Slovakia is expected to join during 2009. There are also five countries where, by formal agreement, the euro is the currency:

➤ Mayotte
➤ Monaco
➤ San Marino
➤ Saint-Pierre-et-Miquelon
➤ Vatican City

And four more where the euro is used without formal agreement:

➢ Akrotiri and Dhekelia   ➢ Kosovo

➢ Andorra   ➢ Montenegro

✳ TIPS ON TIPPING ✳

Many people object to tipping and believe businesses such as hotels and restaurants should state the full price, inclusive of service, at the outset. However, tipping is a fact of life in many countries and you should budget accordingly.

Customs vary in different countries but in general:

➢ Check the bill to see if service has already been included – this is obligatory in some countries.

➢ If service *has* been included, tipping is entirely a matter of personal appreciation – some small change up to a maximum of 5% of the bill; if you've had exceptional service tip towards the higher end but if you've had poor service don't tip at all.

➢ If service *hasn't* been included, a tip of 10 to 15% of a restaurant bill would be about right in most countries. Remember that, whatever you may think of the practice, many employees do rely on tips in order to earn a reasonable living.

➢ In the USA, tips are more frequent and larger than in Europe – the norm is 15 to 20% in restaurants, 10 to 15% in bars and cafés, and 10% at buffets.

➢ In money terms, tips should be relative to the level of earnings in the country, not to the level in the UK.

➢ You don't tip the owner of a restaurant.

TRICKS OF THE TRADE

According to the Center For Hospitality Research at Cornell University in the USA, we're all likely to tip more if a waiter:

➤ Touches us on the shoulder

➤ Squats down by the table when taking an order, thus making level eye contact

➤ Is exceptionally helpful

➤ Presents sweets or chocolate with the bill.

TIPPING ROUND THE WORLD

Rule of thumb ☼

In the USA, these would be the normal tips:
- *Bellhop: $1 per bag (more in a luxury hotel)*
- *Maid: $1 to $10 per night, depending on the room rate*
- *Concierge: $5 to $10 and up to $25 for a special service such as booking a table at a hard-to-get-into restaurant*
- *Doorman: $1 for hailing a taxi*
- *Skycap (porter at an airport): $1 to $2 per bag*
- *Taxi driver: 15 to 20% of the fare*

There isn't space here to give details for every country. Put 'tipping' and the name of your destination into an internet search engine and you'll find plenty of advice. For the experiences of other travellers see www.tripadvisor.com.

In some countries and in certain circumstances personal gifts may be preferred over cash – for example, wine, chocolate, books, lipstick or pens. Check before you travel and buy in the UK if the items are difficult to obtain or expensive in your destination.

Expert's tip ✦

Anywhere in the world that Western tourists visit in large numbers, tipping will be the norm in hotels and restaurants.

TIPPING ON CRUISE SHIPS

At one time tipping on cruise ships was a well-organised routine. On some cruise lines envelopes were provided for the cash to be handed out to the various members of staff. But many companies have now gone over to a system of adding a flat daily charge to the bill (often around £5 a head). In addition, a percentage is often added automatically to extras – for example, 15% to bar bills. Even so, tips will generally be expected for exceptional service, especially by your cabin steward and your waiter.

MOTORING

✳ CAR HIRE ✳

Don't book with the first hire company. Shop around for the best deal. If you have access to the internet use one of the specialist sites such as:

➤ www.carrentals.co.uk
➤ www.holidayautos.co.uk

When you collect your car:

➤ Be sure you understand the fuel situation. Do you have to return the car with a full tank? If you do, ask where the nearest petrol station is before driving away – on the return you may be in a hurry and unable to locate it.

➤ Make sure the insurance covers you for where you intend to go and what you intend to do. Can you cross a frontier, for example, or drive on dirt tracks?

➤ Be sure about the excess situation. Zero doesn't always mean zero as you might still be required to pay for damaged tyres or windscreen.

➤ Find out what to do in the case of a breakdown. With some hire companies you're on your own unless you've paid extra for breakdown cover.

➤ Check the car for existing damage before you drive off.

➤ Be careful not to return the car late – you may be charged for a whole extra day.

HIRE CAR INSURANCE

When you hire a car you're normally responsible for paying an 'excess' if the car is damaged or stolen; that is to say, the first part of the cost up to a certain level. For an extra fee car hire companies offer their own additional insurance to reduce the excess or even set it at zero. But if you often hire cars it may be more economical for you to decline the car hire company's own excess and take out your own annual policy.

Companies offering this include:

➤ www.insurance4carhire.com
➤ www.carhireexcess.com

MAKING A CLAIM

If the car is damaged or stolen the car hire company will debit your credit card up to the level of the excess. You then claim that back from your insurance company.

✷ DRIVING ABROAD ✷

If you don't know the law in the country you're visiting here are some rules that will help you stay safe:

➤ Everyone should wear a seatbelt.

➤ Children under 12 shouldn't ride in the front.

➤ The car should be equipped with replacement bulbs, two warning triangles and two reflective jackets/waistcoats (in the case of breakdown or accident, passengers without reflective jackets/waistcoats should keep out of the road).

➤ If you need glasses to drive you should carry a spare pair.

➤ Don't use a mobile phone while driving.

✳ MOTORING ORGANISATIONS ✳

➤ www.theaa.com – In addition to the well-known breakdown cover, membership of the AA entitles you to a range of discounts on things like car hire, airport parking, car servicing and ferry crossings.

➤ www.arceurope.com – ARC Europe is the creation of eight European automobile clubs to gain more influence and purchasing power. If you're a member of the AA you're automatically a member of ARC (it's on the back of your AA membership card), entitling you to various travel discounts.

✳ DRIVING REGULATIONS ABROAD ✳

Below you'll find country by country regulations on International Driving Permits, alcohol levels and speed limits. Further details of driving regulations are available at www.theaa.com.

INTERNATIONAL DRIVING PERMIT

You can apply for an International Driving Permit:

➤ At selected post offices
➤ At the AA office at Dover Eastern Docks (if travelling by ferry)
➤ At the AA office at Folkestone (if travelling by Eurotunnel)
➤ By post from the AA

For details see www.theaa.com.

International Driving Permits are mostly of the 1949 model but some countries still use the 1926 model:

IDP 1926
Brazil
Burundi (recommended)
Iraq
Somalia

IDP 1949
Afghanistan
Albania
Algeria
Angola (for car hire or for UK licences without a photo)
Argentina
Armenia
Australia (recommended)
Bahrain (go to police to be issued with visitor's licence)
Bangladesh (recommended)
Belarus
Benin
Bhutan
Bolivia
Bosnia (recommended)
Botswana (essential for car hire and recommended for all)
Brunei (essential for car hire and recommended for all)
Bulgaria
Burkino Faso (recommended)
Cambodia
Cameroon (recommended)
Canada (recommended)
Cape Verde (recommended)
Cayman Islands
Central African Republic

Chad
Chile
Colombia
Comoros
Congo Democratic Republic of
Congo Republic of (recommended)
Côte d'Ivoire
Curaçao
Czech Republic (for licences without photograph)
Ecuador (recommended)
Egypt
Equatorial Guinea (recommended)
Eritrea (recommended)
Gabon (for licences without photograph)
Georgia (for licences without photograph)
Ghana (essential for car hire and recommended for all)
Guam
Guinea Bissau (recommended)
Guinea Republic (recommended)
Haiti (recommended)
Hong Kong (recommended)
Hungary (recommended for licences without photograph)
Iceland (recommended for licences without photograph)
India
Indonesia (IDP must be certified by Indonesian Motor
    Association on arrival)
Iran
Israel (essential for car hire and recommended for all)
Italy (recommended for licences without photograph)
Japan
Jordan
Kazakhstan (recommended)
Kenya (recommended)

Korea South
Kuwait
Kyrgyzstan (recommended)
Laos (recommended)
Lebanon
Lesotho (recommended)
Macao
Malaysia (essential for car hire and recommended for all)
Mexico (essential for car hire and recommended for all)
Montenegro (recommended)
Myanmar (police will issue a visitor's licence)
Namibia (essential for licences without photograph and
    recommended for all)
Nepal (IDP valid 15 days after which local licence must be
    obtained)
Niger (recommended)
Nigeria
Oman (police will issue a visitor's licence)
Pakistan
Peru (for stays longer than 30 days)
Philippines (for car hire)
Portugal (recommended for licences without photograph)
Qatar
Romania (for licences without photograph)
Russian Federation
Rwanda (essential for licences without photograph and
    recommended for all)
San Marino (for licences without photograph)
Sao Tome and Principe (recommended)
Saudi Arabia (recommended – note that women aren't allowed
    to drive)
Senegal
Serbia (recommended)

Seychelles (for car hire)
Sierra Leone
Slovakia (for car hire)
Slovenia (essential for licences without photograph and
   recommended for all)
South Africa (essential for car hire and recommended for all)
Spain (recommended for licences without photograph)
Sri Lanka (IDP must be accompanied by certificate from the AA
   in Colombo)
Sudan (recommended)
Surinam
Swaziland (for licences without a photograph)
Syria
Taiwan
Tanzania (recommended – apply to police for a visitor's licence)
Thailand
Togo
Tunisia (recommended for licences without photograph)
Turkey (for licences without a photograph)
Ukraine
UAE
USA (recommended)
Vietnam (recommended – apply to police for a visitor's licence)
Yemen
Zambia (recommended)
Zimbabwe (essential for licences without photograph and
   recommended for all)

ALCOHOL

Country	Maximum Blood Alcohol Concentration %*
Albania	0.01
Argentina	0.05
Australia	0.05

Country	Maximum Blood Alcohol Concentration %*
Austria	0.05
Bahrain	0.00
Belarus	0.04
Belgium	0.05
Belize	0.08
Bosnia Herzegovina	0.05
Brazil	0.08
Bulgaria	0.05
Canada	0.08
Chile	0.08
China	0.03
Croatia	0.05
Cyprus	0.05
Czech Republic	0.00
Denmark	0.05
Ecuador	0.08
Finland	0.05
France	0.05
Georgia	0.03
Germany	0.05
Ghana	0.08
Greece	0.05
Hungary	0.00
Iceland	0.05
India	0.03/0.015
Ireland	0.08
Israel	0.05
Italy	0.05
Jamaica	0.08
Japan	0.03
Jordan	0.00
Latvia	0.05
Lithuania	0.04
Luxembourg	0.08
Macedonia	0.05

Country	Maximum Blood Alcohol Concentration %*
Malaysia	0.08
Malta	0.08
Mauritius	0.08
Moldova	0.03
Monaco	0.05
Namibia	0.05
Netherlands	0.05
New Zealand	0.08
Norway	0.02
Pakistan	0.00
Poland	0.02
Portugal	0.05
Romania	0.00
Russia	0.05
Saudi Arabia	0.00
Serbia	0.05
Singapore	0.08
Slovakia	0.00
Slovenia	0.05
South Africa	0.05
South Korea	0.05
Spain	0.05
Sweden	0.02
Switzerland	0.05
Tanzania	0.08
Thailand	0.05
Turkey	0.05
UAE	0.00
UK	0.08
USA	0.08

Note: A blood alcohol concentration of 0.05% is equivalent to 50 milligrams of alcohol per 100 millilitres of blood.

Rule of thumb ☀

It's impossible to say exactly how much you can drink before you exceed the legal limit because it varies according to weight, sex, speed of consumption, what food you've eaten and your personal metabolism but, as a guide, 0.05% would be roughly equivalent to one pint of low-strength beer or one 125 ml glass of normal-strength wine.

Expert's tip ✦

Many popular destinations have lower alcohol limits than the UK and the penalties can be severe. The best advice is not to drink and drive at all when abroad.

SPEED LIMITS

EU

Km/hr

Country	Built-up areas	Outside built-up areas	Motorways
Austria	50	100	130
Belgium	50	90 or 120	120
Cyprus	50	80	100
Czech Republic	50	90	130
Germany	50	100	130*
Denmark	50	80	110
Spain	50	90 or 100	120
Estonia	50	90 or 100	-
France	50	90 or 110	130 (110 in rain)
Finland	50	80 or 100	120
UK	48 (30 mph)	96 or 112 / 60 or 70 mph	112 / 70 mph
Greece	50	90 or 110	120
Hungary	50	90 or 110	130
Italy	50	90 or 110	130

Country	Built-up areas	Outside built-up areas	Motorways
Ireland	50	80 or 100	120
Luxembourg	50	90	130
Lithuania	50	90 or 100	-
Latvia	50	90 or 100	110 or 130
Malta	50	80	-
Netherlands	50	80 or 100	120
Poland	60	90	130
Portugal	50	90 or 100	120
Sweden	50	70	110
Slovakia	60	90	130
Slovenia	50	90 or 100	130

* Recommended

USA

M/hr

State	Rural interstates	Urban interstates	Other limited access roads	Other roads
Alabama	70	65	65	65
Alaska	65	55	65	55
Arizona	75	65	55	55
Arkansas	70	55	60	55
California	70	65	70	65
Colorado	75	65	65	65
Connecticut	65	55	65	55
Delaware	65	55	65	55
District of Columbia	n/a	55	n/a	25
Florida	70	65	70	65
Georgia	70	65	65	65
Hawaii	60	50	45	45
Idaho	75	75	65	65
Illinois	65	55	65	55
Indiana	70	55	60	55
Iowa	70	55	70	55
Kansas	70	70	70	65
Kentucky	65 or 70	65	65	55

State	Rural interstates	Urban interstates	Other limited access roads	Other roads
Louisiana	70	70	70	65
Maine	65	65	65	60
Maryland	65	65	65	55
Massachusetts	65	65	65	55
Michigan	70	65	70	55
Minnesota	70	65	65	55
Mississippi	70	70	70	65
Missouri	70	60	70	65
Montana	75	65	70 (65 at night)	70 (65 at night)
Nebraska	75	65	65	60
Nevada	75	65	70	70
NewHampshire	65	65	55	55
New Jersey	65	55	65	55
New Mexico	75	75	65	55
New York	65	65	65	55
North Carolina	70	70	70	55
North Dakota	75	75	70	65
Ohio	65	65	55	55
Oklahoma	75	70	70	70
Oregon	65	55	55	55
Pennsylvania	65	55	65	55
Rhode Island	65	55	55	55
SouthCarolina	70	70	60	55
South Dakota	75	75	70	70
Tennessee	70	70	70	65
Texas	75 (65 night)	70 (65 night)	75 (65 night)	60 (55 night)
Utah	75	65	75	65
Vermont	65	55	50	50
Virginia	65	65	65	55
Washington	70	60	60	60
West Virginia	70	55	65	55

| Wisconsin | 65 | 65 | 65 | 55 |
| Wyoming | 75 | 60 | 65 | 65 |

CANADA

Km/hr

	Rural highways	Highways	Towns
	100	80	50

PACKAGE HOLIDAYS

Generally, a package will be cheaper than the same holiday organised independently. The big travel companies have far more muscle than you when it comes to negotiating prices. So, unless you already know you have some pretty special requirements it will pay you to look through the tour operators' brochures and websites.

✳ NEGOTIATING THE BEST PRICE ✳

Package holiday prices can vary considerably between companies and from month to month so, if you want to get the best deal, be prepared to spend time comparing prices. Here are a few tips:

➤ Avoid peaks

➤ Go during school term-time

➤ Opt for a less fashionable destination

➤ www.beatthebrochure.com – claims to help get you better than the brochure price

➤ www.directline-holidays.co.uk – internet holiday search engine

➤ www.holidayhypermarket.co.uk – bargains from leading tour operators

➤ www.lastminute.com – probably the best-known name in travel deals

➤ www.travelcareonline.com – cheap holidays from the Co-op

➤ www.travelsupermarket.com – independent price comparisons

➤ www.teletextholidays.co.uk – cheap holidays, last minute deals, cruises and flights.

Expert's tip ✦

Some agents advertise that they'll try to beat any quote. So get the best price you can and then challenge them to do better.

✳ BOOKING LATE VERSUS ✳ BOOKING EARLY

Which is better?

➤ If you're not insistent on going to a particular hotel in a particular place then you'll get your best deal at the last minute by being flexible.

➤ If it's important to have everything exactly as you've dreamed it, book nine months to one year ahead and get an early-booking discount as well as a full range of choice.

➤ If you book between the two extremes you'll probably end up paying the highest price.

PETS

Everybody worries when a pet is left behind, and that can spoil the trip. On the other hand, taking a dog or cat with you can create its own problems. Here are some tips to help.

✳ GOING ABROAD – ✳ THE LEGAL SITUATION

You can take your cat or dog with you to most European and some non-European countries under the Pet Travel Scheme (PETS).

In order to be eligible your cat or dog will require:

➤ A microchip

➤ A vaccination against rabies

➤ A blood test to show the vaccine is providing satisfactory protection against rabies*

➤ A pet passport

Before returning to the UK your pet will have to be treated for tapeworm and ticks by a vet. This has to be done not less than 24 hours and not more than 48 hours before checking in with your carrier.

* Note that your pet can't re-enter the UK until six months have passed since a satisfactory blood test (which can't be carried out until a sufficient interval after the vaccination), so you'll need to start all this at least seven months in advance.

Only PET-approved rail, sea or air carriers can be used. Animals arriving on yachts or private aircraft will not be eligible.

For further information:

➢ www.defra.gov.uk 08459 335577 – site includes details of approved routes and carriers

➢ PETS helpline 0870 241 1710

✳ TRANSPORTING YOUR PET ✳

YOUR PET IN THE CAR

Many dogs enjoy car journeys. However, your pet should not be allowed to travel on your lap or stick its head out of the window. You are risking your pet's safety if they do, as well as your own – in an accident, an unrestrained animal can become a missile.

➢ Your pet should be restrained, just as you are, in case you should make an emergency stop – or worse; use a proper pet seatbelt and harness combination.

➢ If your pet is in a travel crate, make sure the crate is secured so it can't move.

➢ Some cats and dogs get car sick so it's usually best that their last meal is several hours before departure.

➢ Take your pet for a good walk before setting off.

➢ Stop every two to three hours so your pet – and you – can have a walk.

➢ If you have to leave your pet in the car alone for a while leave the windows open enough for good ventilation.

➢ Never leave an animal in a car in direct sunshine – even with the windows open a car can quickly heat up to a dangerous temperature.

YOUR PET BY TRAIN

Dogs and cats are allowed on most trains in the UK and Europe. Often they travel free, but must not occupy a seat. Large dogs are usually charged half fare. Unless in a container, dogs must be kept on a lead. Check with the individual operators. The major exception is that pets are not allowed on Eurostar, which means that foot passengers with their pets have to travel between the UK and the Continent on ferries that have on-board kennels (see below).

Expert's tip ✦

If you want a sleeper compartment to get a good night's rest your party will have to book all the berths (so there's no risk of your dog disturbing other passengers). You may also have to pay an extra cleaning charge.

YOUR PET BY COACH

Generally, pets (other than guide dogs) are not allowed on buses and coaches in the UK, or on Eurolines coaches to other European destinations. However, some operators do allow drivers to use their discretion. On the Continent the rules vary so check with the individual operators.

YOUR PET BY AIR

Different airlines have different policies but, in general, in the UK and on international routes to and from the UK, only guide/assistance dogs are allowed in the cabin. However, some airlines will allow small cats and dogs (usually 5kg or less) to travel in the cabin in a container. American airlines are more easy going on domestic routes, allowing small animals in suitable containers to be stowed under the seats.

All other dogs and cats will travel in the hold. That may not sound very nice but it will be temperature-controlled and although it will be dark most animals do, in fact, travel better that way. There are two methods:

➤ Your pet travels on the same aircraft as you, as 'accompanied baggage'.

➤ Your pet travels separately, as cargo.

Note that the cost of flying as cargo will be several times higher than the cost of flying as accompanied baggage.

You'll need an IATA-approved travel box with the following features:

➤ It must have ventilation on all four sides but be impossible for your pet to push a paw or nose out through it

➤ There must be a food container and water container *accessible from outside*.

➤ It must be large enough for your pet to be able to stand up, turn around and lie down comfortably.

You can see the detailed specification at:
www.iata.org/whatwedo/cargo/live_animals/pets.htm

The easiest solution is to buy a container ready-made to IATA specifications rather than try to make your own.

Note that many airlines have temperature restrictions and will not accept animals as cargo if the temperature at either the departure or arrival airport is too high or too low.

YOUR PET ON THE FERRY

Again, different companies have different policies but, normally, only guide dogs are allowed on the passenger decks. Some ferry operators won't allow foot passengers to bring pets at all and insist on motorists leaving their pets in the car, with no access during the crossing.

P&O Ferries may allow foot passengers to bring cats and small dogs if kept in an approved carrrier at all times. Pets are not allowed at all on the Bilbao crossing.

➤ www.poferries.com 08716 645 645

StenaLine may have car-deck kennels which you *will* be allowed to visit, at the discretion of the staff. Foot passengers can take cats and dogs on the Harwich to Hook of Holland route – small pets must be kept in a travel box; larger dogs must be booked in to the onboard kennels.

➤ www.stenaline.co.uk 08705 70 70 70

Brittany Ferries carries around 30,000 dogs and cats a year. The Pont Aven, which makes the 19-and-a-half hour crossing from Plymouth to Santander, has 42 kennels in a special area on one of the upper decks. There you can visit your pet as often as you like.

➤ www.brittanyferries.com 08705 360 360

YOUR PET AND ACCOMMODATION

Some hotels and self-catering units allow pets and others don't, so check at the time of booking.

➤ If you think you may have to leave your pet alone in the room for a while then you should have a travel container, to avoid damage to the room.

➤ Don't leave your dog alone if he barks. If you're not sure how your dog will react to your absence, just go outside for a few minutes and listen.

➢ Some animals find it relaxing to have the radio or TV on quietly.

➢ Make sure you clean up after your dog.

➢ Hang the *Do Not Disturb* sign on the door.

➢ If you intend to take your pet away for a week or two and you've never done it before, have a one-night test run in a hotel beforehand.

Some useful websites:

➢ www.petplanet.co.uk – Information on pet-friendly accommodation in the UK and Europe.

➢ www.dogsinvited.co.uk – Pet-friendly accommodation in the UK only.

➢ www.k9directory.co.uk – Pet-friendly accommodation in the UK only.

➢ www.pettravel.com – American site which gives details of pet-friendly accommodation in many other countries as well.

And a useful book:

Pet Friendly Places To Stay, AA Publishing, 2007. Paperback guide to suitable UK accommodation.

✳ PET TRAVEL AGENTS ✳

Yes, Fido can have his own special travel agent to take care of all the arrangements (and, in fact, some countries insist on them).

➢ www.airpets.com 0800 371 554 or 01753 685 571

➤ www.skydogs.co.uk 01629 734 000
➤ www.passportforpets.co.uk 0800 137 321
➤ www.ladyhaye.co.uk 01342 832161

✳ GENERAL ADVICE ✳

➤ Take plenty of water with you for the journey.

➤ Give your dog a good walk before joining the queue to get on the ferry or whatever.

➤ Take something familiar for your pet – a blanket or toy.

➤ Take a supply of your pet's usual food so that food bought abroad can be introduced gradually.

Expert's tip ✦

♦ In case your pet should get lost, have a collar tag made giving your pet's name and your mobile telephone number, as dialled from the country you're visiting.

♦ When travelling with a cat by air, train or coach it can be useful to create your own collapsible litter tray. Here's how. Get as many large, sturdy bin bags as you think you'll need, cut them down to a suitable height, put sufficient cat litter in each one, secure the tops and stow in your luggage. When you think the litter 'tray' is needed just spread the bag open. Once used, tie the bag up and put in a rubbish bin. If you have space in your luggage, you can improve the design by using the lid of a shoe box to strengthen the tray. It's a good idea to get your cat used to this arrangement at home beforehand.

RESEARCHING AND EXPLORING

✳ GUIDEBOOKS AND ✳ ELECTRONIC GUIDES

There's not a great deal to say about conventional guidebooks. As with teabags, everyone has their favourite brand. But while a printed guidebook still has a role there are modern alternatives.

Expert's tip ✦

♦ Guidebook writers can't know everything and usually appreciate feedback from readers. So make notes about any errors or omissions and send them in – you might be rewarded by a copy of the next edition.

♦ If your guidebook is already a bit dog-eared check the publisher's website for updates.

YOUR MOBILE PHONE

You can have travel information downloaded to your mobile phone. Concierge.com, for example, can send you information about hotels and restaurants. To select downloads go to their website:

➤ www.concierge.com/services/mobile

AUDIO GUIDES AND PODCASTS

In some destinations and in many museums you can now rent portable audio guides that will take you on a tour and explain what you're looking at. One of the latest versions is the podcast. Podcasts are distributed over the internet for you to listen to on your portable computer or MP3 player (portable music player). Increasingly there are video podcasts, too. Some are designed for you to listen to before you go while others will actually take you around – you listen to the directions on your MP3 player, turn it off until you reach the point of interest, turn it on to hear the commentary when you arrive … and so on and so on.

Here are some internet sites from which you can download:

➤ www.digitalpodcast.com/browse.travel-31-1.html – directory of travel podcasts

➤ www.podcast.net/cat/39 – directory of travel podcasts

➤ www.independent.co.uk/travel/the-independents-travel-podcast-service – guide to major cities round the world

➤ www.travelin10.libsyn.com – 10-minute audio tours

➤ www.lonelyplanet.com/travelstories/podcast/ – travel podcasts from Lonely Planet

➤ www.roughguides.com/podcasts/ – podcasts from Rough Guides

➤ www.wildebeat.net – wilderness travel

➤ www.itoors.com – the trendy side of the world's major cities

Expert's tip ✦

Get your bearings on a tourist bus such as the open-top double-decker tours around London. Most large cities have them and many operate a system of hop on/off tickets. Later you can go back and take a closer look at the things that interest you.

GPS

Nowadays there's much more to GPS (Global Positioning System) than simply telling you where you are. The most advanced models will:

➢ Show you where the nearest ATMs, restaurants, hotels, hospitals, petrol stations, police stations and points of interest are.

➢ Lead you where you want to go.

➢ Add hands-free capability to your mobile phone.

➢ Alert you to traffic jams and provide an alternative route.

➢ Provide you with travel information and recommendations for hotels, restaurants, nightlife, shopping and tourist attractions.

If you decide to buy GPS (but you can rent – see below) you can choose between:

➢ Handheld

➢ In-car navigation systems (also called called SatNav)

➢ GPS software for your existing GPS-enabled mobile phone or Personal Digital Assistant (PDA).

For further information see:

➢ www.which.co.uk – consumer advice
➢ http://gpsprimer.net – GPS basics

➤ www.gpsw.co.uk – GPS Warehouse
➤ www.sciuridae.co.uk – online specialist magazine

Expert's tip ✦

♦ Clouds, rain or snow will not affect the performance or the accuracy of GPS but a roof or even a thick tree canopy can.

♦ Only the most sophisticated GPS systems have a built-in compass so, for wilderness travel, take one with you.

♦ Your GPS will initially take some time to find the satellites so switch on well before you actually need it.

♦ Don't put all your eggs in one GPS receiver. You may run out of battery power, an elephant may tread on it or you may fall into the river.

♦ For some extra fun with your GPS try geocaching. It's a virtual treasure hunt to find a real or virtual cache of treasure and it's played all over the globe.

RENTING GPS

▌ *Rule of thumb* ☼
  GPS is normally accurate to around 50'/15 m.

You don't have to buy a GPS if you're only going to use it on holiday or on a business trip. If you're hiring a car you can usually get it as an extra or put 'GPS rental' into your search engine or see:

➤ www.roadmate.co.uk – rent by the day or longer for the UK and Europe

➤ www.gpsplanet.com – GPS rental in Europe, North America and more

➤ www.cheapsatnavhire.co.uk – good value rental for Europe, North America and more

WEBCAMS

In 1991 some people in the computer science department of Cambridge University pointed a camera at their coffee pot and hooked it up to the world wide web. Thus the first webcam was born and the coffee pot was its first star, appearing daily for 10 years.

It may seem unbelievable but there are now literally millions of similar webcams set up all over the world. They point at famous buildings, busy streets, quiet streets, mountains, beaches, ski resorts, dance floors, people's dogs and much, much more. In other words, on your computer, you can connect to remote cameras in a mind-boggling variety of places to see what's going on. Right now.

Which means you can use webcams to:

➤ Decide whether or not you want to visit an area, resort, town, museum or entertainment.

➤ See what conditions are like (for example, which ski resort has the best snow or how many people are on the beach).

➤ Identify something you're not sure of.

➤ See when a contact has arrived.

Let's say, for example, you're staying in an area where you have a choice of ski resorts to go to. Normally you'd check the snow reports. But how reliable are they? With a webcam you can judge the snow for yourself and, what's more, see how busy each resort is.

All you have to do is sit in front of your laptop, access an index of webcams and click on the ones in the target area. With luck there may be several and you'll be able to make an informed judgement before setting off.

And how exactly do you do this? It's very simple. Once connected to the internet just put the destination into your search engine together with the word 'webcam' and see what comes up. Alternatively, you can go to a webcam index to see what's listed. Here are a few to get you started:

> www.earthcam.com
> www.camcentral.com
> www.webcam-index.com
> www.webcamsearch.com
> www.webcamworld.com

You can also see satellite images of most places on Earth in incredible detail at:

> http://earth.google.com/

VIRTUAL TOURS

Another way to check a place out is the virtual tour, again available via your computer. Some provide a series of still pictures, some provide 360° panoramas and some – the best – are short videos. Put 'virtual tour' and the name of your destination into your search engine or take a look at:

> www.concierge.com

> www.virtualfreesites.com – directory of virtual sites

> www.youtube.com – No, it's not all teenagers doing daft things. In fact, if you've never tried it you'll be amazed. Just select 'video' and type in the name of the destination or building you want to see. With luck, you'll be offered several different videos, usually lasting three to five minutes, made by people who have been there.

FEEDBACK

It's always useful to hear what other people think of a place, hotel or restaurant. For feedback take a look at:

➢ www.tripadvisor.com

➢ www.reviewcentre.com

➢ www.thisistravel.com

Expert's tip ✦

If you have a particular hobby and are a member of a club at home, get in touch with the equivalent organisation in your destination. You should be able to get a contact address through your own national association.

✳ HUMAN GUIDES ✳

If you don't have time to plan, or simply like the idea of placing yourself in the hands of an expert, try putting 'private guide' into your search engine together with the name of your destination. You can hire a professional guide for a couple of hours to show you round a museum or for the entire duration of your stay. In Europe guides usually charge around £200 to £250 a day but many other parts of the world will be cheaper. Long journeys in the guide's own car will cost extra.

➢ www.blue-badge-guides.com – site for The Guild of Registered Tourist Guides which maintains a directory of "Blue Badge" guides working in the UK. 020 7403 1115.

➢ www.londoncountrytours.co.uk – London and Britain. 020 8642 2193

➢ www.private-guides.com – Online directory of travel guides worldwide.

➢ www.privateguidesineurope.com – Online directory of travel guides in Europe.

Expert's tip ✦

Before booking, check that a guide is qualified (with a Blue Badge in the UK, for example) and licensed by the local tourist office.

If you intend to book a guide in advance for several days, talk on the telephone at least twice to make sure you're going to get on.

✳ MAPS AND MAP READING ✳

There's still a role for old-fashioned paper maps, especially for hikers. They contain a vast amount of information – if you know how to read them.

First the contour lines:

➤ If the contour lines are close together the terrain is steep.

➤ If the contour lines are far apart the terrain is gentle.

➤ If the path follows the contour line then it is neither ascending nor descending.

➤ If the path cuts across contour lines then it is either ascending or descending.

Next, distance:

➤ Take a piece of cotton, lay it out along the path marked on the map and then measure it off along the scale printed on the map.

➤ Flat maps can't take into account the extra distance walked as the ground climbs and falls so add about 5% in mountainous areas.

➤ Add another 5% for all the little wiggles too small to measure.

HOW FAR CAN I GO?

Rule of thumb ☼

For hiking purposes you need a scale of either:
- *1:25,000 which means 1cm on the map represents 250m on the ground*
- *1:50,000 which means 1cm on the map represents 500m on the ground*

If you're walking, cycling or swimming for pleasure on holiday these are the kinds of speeds you can expect:

➢ Walking – about 4kph/2.5mph on the flat over the course of a day; add an hour for every 300m/1000ft of ascent.

➢ Cycling – about 16kph/10mph on the flat over the course of a day; in hilly terrain increase times by about a quarter.

➢ Swimming – about 1.5kph/1mph.

Expert's tip ✦
- ◆ Get used to your map before you need it. Spread it out on the table or floor at home and pore over it. Check the key then try to visualise the terrain in your mind – the fields, trees, rocky outcrops, streams, gradients and so on.
- ◆ The heights of the main (thicker) contour lines are marked on them somewhere but it isn't always easy to find the numbers to see whether the ground is rising or falling. But in most areas you can tell at a glance by the streams, which can only run in the valley bottoms, not on the ridges.

Rule of thumb ☼

Times given on hiking signs or in guidebooks don't normally allow for rest stops, so increase them by between a fifth and a third, depending on your level of fitness.

15

SECURITY

When travelling you're almost always at greater risk than in your daily life. You'll be exposed to situations where you won't know what's normal and what's not normal. You'll almost certainly be carrying more valuables than local people, and there are criminals who make a point of preying on tourists. But you don't want to spoil your trip constantly worrying about these things. Make security measures a routine – just like looking before crossing the road – and enjoy yourself.

First, some general tips:

➤ Try not to look like a tourist
➤ Try not to look 'lost'
➤ Aim to look confident and purposeful
➤ Always be alert for suspicious people
➤ Avoid being out late at night
➤ Avoid areas known to be dangerous

✳ DANGEROUS PLACES ✳

Countries or areas considered dangerous are listed in travel advisories by the British government. Obviously it's safer to avoid them unless there's some compelling reason to go.

Specifically as regards terrorism, the government has four levels:

➤ A high threat from terrorism

➤ A general threat from terrorism

➤ An underlying threat from terrorism

➤ A low threat from terrorism

The meanings aren't very specific but you get the general idea.

Only very rarely does the government advise British nationals against *all* travel to a country, so such warnings should be treated very seriously. At the time of writing, the FCO advised against *all* travel to only one country which was:

➤ Somalia

To check out travel advisories:

➤ www.fco.gov.uk 0845 850 2829 (24/7; calls charged at 4p/minute)

➤ From abroad you should call 00 44 1530 553424 (Mon – Fri 8am – 8pm) or 00 44 2891 476 754 (outside normal UK hours).

➤ You might also like to check with the USA State Department at http://travel.state.gov/

At the time of writing, the State Department considered the following countries to be dangerous: Afghanistan, Algeria, Burundi, Central African Republic, Chad, Columbia, Côte d'Ivoire, Democratic Republic of the Congo, Eritrea, Gaza, Haiti, Indonesia, Iran, Iraq, Israel, Kenya, Lebanon, Nigeria, Nepal, Pakistan, Philippines, Saudi Arabia, Somalia, Sri Lanka, Sudan, Syria, Timor-Leste, Uzbekistan, the West Bank, Yemen.

To that list we would add: Liberia and Zimbabwe.

And here are the most dangerous cities in the world:

➤ Port Moresby, Papua New Guinea
➤ Karachi, Pakistan
➤ Dhaka, Bangladesh
➤ Lagos, Nigeria
➤ Phnom Penh, Cambodia

(If you'd like to know the safest cities, they're considered to be: Melbourne, Australia; Vancouver, Canada; Vienna, Austria; Perth, Australia; Geneva, Switzerland.)

Expert's tip ➤

When you're in a strange city ask someone in your hotel or any local contact if there are any areas you should avoid – and avoid them.

✳ LUGGAGE SECURITY ✳

Luggage security begins at home when you do your packing:

➤ Use plain, sturdy but inexpensive suitcases.

➤ Make a list of important items in your luggage and photograph them.

➤ Put your full contact details, including the hotels you'll be staying at and the dates, on a sheet of card inside your suitcase, so you can easily be contacted if you and your luggage get separated.

➤ Put a luggage strap around the case both to identify it on the luggage carousel (if flying) and to prevent it bursting open with rough handling.

➤ Put your name on a luggage tag together with your mobile number but not your home address or home telephone number.

➤ Photocopy important documents such as passports and leave one copy with relatives or friends.

Expert's tip ✦

Lock your suitcase with a TSA lock, not just to protect the contents but to make sure no one slips drugs or anything else inside. These locks can be opened by members of the Transport Security Administration in the USA so that, if a hand search is carried out, neither the lock nor the suitcase gets damaged. They're being increasingly accepted elsewhere. TSA locks can be bought online from www.tamperseal.com.

Keep valuables, documents, medicines and essentials with you in your hand luggage when flying or travelling by train, coach or ferry. When sitting with your hand luggage or handbag (at an airport café, for example) put your leg or the chair leg through the straps. A motion-sensing alarm is also a good idea. They're available from specialist shops and online from companies such as www.catch22products.co.uk 01942 511 820.

✳ HOTEL SECURITY ✳

There are two kinds of robberies in hotels. Firstly there are day-time burglaries in which the thief hopes you won't be in your room. Then there are so-called 'room invasions' at night in which two or more criminals plan not only to rob you but also to intimidate you into handing over credit cards and revealing your PIN codes.

➤ Don't have expensive luggage.

➤ Don't hire an expensive car.

➤ Don't flash large sums of money.

➤ Don't wear expensive jewellery.

➤ Don't go to your room if someone suspicious gets into the lift with you, or follows you along a corridor; return to the lobby instead.

➤ Don't open the door to anyone without checking identity first.

➤ Don't open the door on the security chain if you're at all suspicious – a determined man may be able to break the fixings.

➤ Don't open the door at all if you haven't requested anyone to come.

➤ Don't hang a 'breakfast request' on the doorknob – a criminal can see at a glance how many people are in the room and pretend to deliver breakfast as a means of gaining access. If you're alone, either go without or order two breakfasts.

➤ Do ask for a room on a higher floor and away from any external stairs (criminals prefer rooms from which there's a quick getaway).

➤ Do keep the room locked and engage the chain or other security device provided.

➤ Do put the 'Do Not Disturb' sign on the door when out and leave the TV or radio on as well as a light (if the energy-saving system permits).

➤ Do ask someone you trust to accompany you to your room if you're a woman travelling alone.

➤ Do have an alarm – there are models that sound when the handle is touched, when a door or window is opened or when anyone moves inside the room.

➤ Do put valuables in the safe in your room – if there isn't one, deter casual thieves by using a portable safe anchored to any sturdy piece of furniture.

Expert's tip ✦

The simplest piece of security equipment is a door wedge to prevent anyone entering your room during the night. You can buy rubber ones very cheaply and they'll slip into a tiny space in your luggage. If you don't have one you might be able to improvise with something in your luggage such as the base of a pocket stapler or even a notebook or a piece of wood picked up outside.

❋ CAR PARKS ❋

Car parks can be dangerous places:

➤ Don't park if you see suspicious people.

➤ If you have parked, don't unlock the doors or get out if there are suspicious people – if necessary, drive off again.

➤ Park your car in the best-lit, most used area of the car park.

➤ Don't leave any valuables on view.

➤ If there's a valet parking system, use it.

➤ If someone suspicious appears to be following you when you return to the car park, don't go to your car but walk briskly to a safe place.

➤ Look around before unlocking your car.

➤ Carry a personal alarm.

❋ SECURITY ON THE STREETS ❋

When you're travelling you'll probably have more documents and valuables with you than at other times so you need to take special precautions.

Women are targeted more often than men, partly because they're less likely to fight back but mostly because snatching one handbag will usually net a thief a wide variety of goodies – cash, credit cards, driving licence, passport, mobile phone, MP3 player and so on. As always, the advice is to spread valuables around and not to have more in your handbag than you really need.

Pickpockets often work in pairs. (Don't assume that only men are pickpockets; women do it, too, *and children*.) One diverts your attention and the other does the stealing. Here are some of the diversionary tactics:

➤ Someone asks you the time or for directions.

➤ Someone, lying on the pavement, grabs your leg.

➤ Someone deliberately picks an argument with you.

In any such situation *think security first* – in other words, secure your handbag or briefcase before telling someone the time.

HANDBAGS

➤ Don't use a backpack-style handbag, unless it's reinforced and lockable – it's too easy for someone to steal something without you even knowing.

➤ Keep your handbag closed.

➤ If you put your bag down put your foot or the leg of your chair through the straps.

➤ Consider using a purpose-made security-style handbag (such as the models made by Pacsafe – see www.pacsafe.com).

MONEY BELTS

Both men and women should wear money belts. The most useful sort go under your clothes, usually with the pocket across your stomach. For aesthetic reasons you probably won't want to put too much inside, but a passport and some folding money won't spoil your silhouette. If you're concerned about that you can also buy holster styles.

Less spacious but even more secret are real belts, worn in the normal way, but with a secret compartment on the inside large enough to take folded paper money.

CLOTHES WITH ZIP POCKETS

Some clothes have zip pockets, especially those expressly made for travelling. See, for example, www.rohan.co.uk.

Expert's tip ✦

Always spread valuables around. Rather than have all your credit/debit cards in one holder use two holders and put them in separate pockets. Wear a money belt. For emergencies, keep some paper money (protected by a small plastic bag) inside your shoe. Women, especially, take note – don't put all your eggs in one handbag.

PERSONAL ALARMS

Get a personal alarm. Look for at least 130db. They're small, light, inexpensive and could save not just your valuables but also your life. Put 'personal alarm' into your search engine or see:

➤ www.amazon.co.uk
➤ www.personalalarms.com 01978 855054
➤ www.catch22products.co.uk 01942 511 820

Expert's tip ✦

Never chase after someone who has stolen your bag or anything else. Don't be a hero. It's just not worth the risk. You could find yourself facing a knife, a gun and maybe a whole gang.

DEALING WITH PERSISTENT STREET VENDORS

Street vendors can completely ruin your enjoyment. But they can also add to it. So it's a question of having a balanced attitude.

➤ Always be respectful, no matter how annoying they are being.

➤ If you have a genuine interest in anything on sale, make the most of the experience.

➤ If you're not interested, be polite but firm and move on.

➤ Always be alert for pickpockets when you're being jostled in a market or in the street.

Expert's tip ✛

It's often a good idea to address a street vendor as 'Sir'. It can smooth away any possible resentments about Westerners and make it easier to get away.

✳ SOME SCAMS TO WATCH ✳ OUT FOR

Good places to learn about scams are www.virtualtourist.com and www.lonelyplanet.com/thorntree. The latter is a travel message board covering all kinds of subjects but if you put in 'scams' (or something like that) together with the name of your destination, you'll be forewarned.

Here are a few:

➤ THE TRAVELCARD SCAM. You're offered a card that identifies you as a travel agent or similar, entitled to free upgrades and other perks. Most of these are worthless, but if you do see such an offer and are interested, check first by telephoning an airline to see if they recognise the card.

➤ THE COMPETITION SCAM. You receive an e-mail, telephone call or letter telling you you've won a travel prize in a competition you've never entered. Ignore such offers (they usually involve you telephoning a number on a premium line).

➤ **THE HARD LUCK STORY**. There are all kinds of variations. Usually, someone claims to have had everything stolen and asks for money to get home.

➤ **THE CHEAP JEWELLERY SCAM**. You're offered a watch, a ring, gold coins or, indeed, just about anything at an incredibly cheap price. Of course, the items are fake or stolen.

➤ **THE FAKE TAXI SCAM**. Someone offers you a cheap taxi service but then takes you on the 'scenic route' and charges you far more than the normal fare. If you refuse to pay, the 'taxi driver' may keep your luggage locked in the boot.

➤ **THE THAI GEM SCAM**. This one is worth relating in some detail because it illustrates how elaborate some scams have become. You hail a taxi or túk-túk (three-wheeled taxi) to visit, say, a temple. The driver tells you your chosen temple is closed but will take you to another. Along the way he mentions in conversation that today is special because (say) taxes on gems have been removed for one day only (for some ridiculous reason). At the temple a stranger strikes up a conversation with you and also just happens to mention the possibility of buying cheap gems. You now ask the túk-túk driver to take you to the gem shop, where you buy a load of worthless junk. (There are variations involving suits and other items, too.)

Expert's tip ✦

♦ If something seems too good to be true it probably is.
♦ Always check your bill, especially after driving a hard bargain. You may find the addition of an unexpected tax, service or delivery charge.

♦ *Never be distracted into taking your eye off your bag or wallet. A favourite trick is to drop your change near your feet and as you bend to retrieve it your belongings are removed.*

MOTORING

Common scams include putting nails in the road to puncture tyres and even spraying your car with paint. The idea is that you'll stop and get out, and while you're distracted the thief or thieves will steal anything of value. If your car is sprayed with paint, ignore it and drive on. If a tyre is punctured and you can't drive on, keep the car locked. Call for help on a mobile, if you have one. Sadly, anybody who offers you help *is probably one of the gang.* Watch out!

✳ WHAT TO DO IF SOMETHING ✳ IS STOLEN

1 The first step has to be taken *before* anything gets stolen. It is to photocopy (both sides) credit cards, driving licences, passports and so on. Keep these copies in a safe place. At the same time record the telephone numbers of organisations that will have to be alerted if anything gets stolen. Make a note of the serial numbers of cameras, mobile phones and so on (and always store purchase receipts in a safe place so you can prove to your insurance company that you had them).

2 Call your credit card companies and report the theft. Make a note of the name of the person you speak to. If you wish you can subscribe to a service that will cancel all your cards for you – you only need to dial one number.

3 Contact the main credit-reporting agencies and ask them to attach a fraud alert to your file:
  ➤ www.callcredit.co.uk

➢ www.equifax.co.uk
➢ www.uk.experian.com

4 If you've lost other important documents (driving licence, passport) you'll have to report these, too.

5 Contact the police.

6 If you experience problems (for example, you see transactions on your credit card statement that weren't made by you) get in touch with CIFAS, the UK's Fraud Prevention Service and ask for Protective Registration. Any financial applications using your address will then be subject to extra security check: www.cifas.org.uk 0870 010 2091 or email protective.registration@equifax.com.

✳ SECURITY ON THE BEACH ✳

When you go to the beach you can be very vulnerable. You may have the keys to your car or hire car with you. You'll probably have some cash. And you may have other valuables, too, such as a camera or mobile phone.

Small items can be stored in a personal 'beach safe' hung round your neck. Look for a design that's truly waterproof and has built-in buoyancy, in case you lose it in the sea. Aquapac makes a waterproof money belt that's guaranteed waterproof to 15 feet (five metres), available from: www.catch22products.co.uk 01942 511 820.

For larger items there are mini safes that can be secured to something solid using a lockable cable (always assuming you can find something suitable on the beach). A new trend is for beaches to be equipped with safe deposit boxes (for example, on Cyprus). Online companies that supply beach safes and related items include:

➤ www.goplanetgo.co.uk
➤ www.walkabouttravelgear.com
➤ www.over-board.co.uk 01932 232 126

✳ BUSINESS TRAVEL SECURITY ✳

Holidaymakers always have a choice but business people some-times have to go where they'd rather not.

➤ Vary your route and your timing every day – never establish a pattern.

➤ Avoid alcohol – it could make a crucial difference to your judgement and your reactions.

➤ Avoid displays of wealth.

➤ Travel in a group whenever possible.

➤ Keep up-to-date with security information.

✳ SECURITY BACK HOME ✳

You know how it is when you're away for a week or two. You have a great time but there's always that nagging little worry there could be a problem at home. When you get back you have to steel yourself before you put the key in the lock, just in case you've been burgled or a water pipe has burst.

Well, no longer. Not if you set up a webcam. Using a laptop or an internet café, you'll be able to see that your favourite antiques are still there, that the storm didn't blow the roof off, and that the neighbour is remembering to feed the cat.

SETTING UP A WEBCAM AT HOME

It's quite easy to create your own webcam set-up, provided you have a high-speed internet connection.

Here are the things that you need:

➤ A fairly modern computer
➤ A high-speed connection
➤ A webcam (a camera connected to your computer)
➤ The software to make the system work

Basic webcams are very cheap (under £20) although, as with most things, you can spend more if you want to. Normally they're attached to the computer via a cable and a USB port (some computers even have them built in). However, if you'd like to be able to move the camera around, you'll need an extra length video cable or, better still, some kind of cable-free set-up such as a home network.

The software will 'grab a frame' from the camera at preset intervals. In a simple system this could be every 30 seconds. Naturally, the higher the rate the faster your connection needs to be.

The images need to be uploaded to a web server such as AOL Instant Messenger, Yahoo Messenger, Windows Live Messenger, Skype, Ekigg or Camfrog.

And that, basically, is all there is to it.

SHOPPING

Abroad you can buy certain things cheaper than at home as well as arts, crafts, foodstuffs and high technology items not available in the UK. But you have to know what you're doing.

❊ ALLOWANCES ❊

There are different allowances for:

➤ Goods purchased in EU countries
➤ Goods purchased outside the EU
➤ Goods purchased in duty free shops

ARRIVING BACK IN THE
UK FROM WITHIN THE EU

ALCOHOL AND TOBACCO

Theoretically, you can bring unlimited amounts of alcohol and tobacco back into the UK if bought tax-paid from shops in other EU countries provided:

➤ It's for your personal consumption or gifts
➤ It travels with you

In reality you'll be questioned very closely if you exceed the following quantities and risk having the items confiscated or worse:

➤ 3,200 cigarettes

➢ 200 cigars
➢ 400 cigarillos
➢ 3kg tobacco
➢ 110 litres of beer
➢ 90 litres of wine
➢ 10 litres of spirits or 20 litres of fortified wine (such as port or sherry).

Note that limits are even lower for alcohol and tobacco bought in some of the newer member states. At the time of writing these countries were:

➢ Estonia – only 200 cigarettes or 250g of smoking tobacco.

➢ Bulgaria, Hungary, Latvia, Lithuania, Poland, Romania or Slovakia – 200 cigarettes but no limit on other tobacco products for your personal use.

The Canary Islands, Channel Islands, Gibraltar and North Cyprus are considered non-EU as regards imports into the UK.

FOOD AND PLANTS

➢ You can bring back a reasonable amount of any food on sale in any EU country for personal use.

➢ Generally, you can bring back plants for your garden as long as they're not endangered but restrictions do apply to certain species – see www.defra.gov.uk.

ARRIVING BACK IN THE UK FROM OUTSIDE THE EU

ALCOHOL, TOBACCO AND PERFUME

You are allowed:

➢ 200 cigarettes or 100 cigarillos or 50 cigars or 250 grams of tobacco

➤ 2 litres still table wine

➤ 1 litre of spirits or 2 litres of fortified wine

➤ 60cc perfume

➤ 250cc eau de toilette

➤ £145 of other goods including gifts and souvenirs

FOOD

You can bring back a reasonable quantity (around 2kgs/4.4lbs) of food except:

➤ Anything of animal origin

➤ Potatoes

However, there are exceptions to the restrictions for certain items including:

➤ Animal products from Andorra, Faroe Islands, Greenland, Iceland, Liechtenstein, Norway, San Marino and Switzerland.

➤ A reasonable amount of shellfish from Norway and Iceland.

➤ Caviar up to 250g for personal consumption (see www.cites.org).

▐ *Rule of thumb* ✺
Exceptions are also made for small amounts of commercial baby food and special foods for medical conditions as long as they're for personal consumption and in the original packaging.

Expert's tip ✦

Restrictions can vary at very short notice so always check with the Department of Environment, Food and Rural Affairs (DEFRA) www.defra.gov.uk 08459 335577; or the Food Standards Agency (FSA) www.food.gov.uk 0207 2768018.

PLANTS

The import of many plants from non-EU countries is either prohibited or requires health certificates. However, small quantities may be imported provided they are:

➤ For your private home or garden
➤ In your personal luggage
➤ Free from signs of pest or disease

Expert's tip ✦

Most, but not all, cut flowers are permitted as are up to five retail packets of seeds (not seeds of potatoes). Always check beforehand with DEFRA (contact details above).

ARRIVING BACK IN THE UK WITH DUTY FREE

Duty and tax free shopping *within* the EU was abolished in 1999 and is now only available to passengers travelling *outside* the EU. When you buy goods in, say, an airport shop while travelling from the UK to another EU country, or back, they're not actually duty or tax free. Some outlets advertise that they pay the tax on your behalf but that's a meaningless phrase because, in effect, all retailers have to do that anyway. The test of whether of not it's worth buying something in an airport shop or on a ferry when travelling within the EU is to compare with high street and internet prices. Some things will be cheaper and some won't.

NOTE: There are some places you may have thought were within the EU, or were covered by EU tax regulations, which are not:

➤ Aland Islands (Finland)

➤ Andorra

➤ Busingen and Helgoland (Germany)

➤ The Canary Islands, Ceuta and Melilla (Spain)

➤ Channel Islands

➤ The comunes of Livigno and Campione d'Italia (Italy)

➤ Faroe Islands and Greenland (Denmark)

➤ Gibraltar

➤ Martinique, French Guiana, Guadeloupe, Reunion, St Pierre and Miquelon (France)

➤ Mount Athos (Greece)

WHAT'S MY ALLOWANCE?

➤ When travelling within the EU there is no duty-free allowance.

➤ When travelling from the UK to a non-EU country your duty-free allowance is determined by the country you're travelling to.

➤ When travelling back to the UK from a non-EU country, any duty-free goods will form part of your total non-EU allowance (see above); you may be asked to pay tax or duty on anything over your allowance.

Expert's tip ✛

♦ Check prices in the high street and from online shops before buying from an airport shop or on a ferry.

♦ Also check the specification carefully – items in duty free shops and high street shops may look the same but they could be different.

♦ Some airports now have shops in the arrivals hall to save you having to carry your purchases on to the plane.

✳ PROHIBITED OR ✳ CONTROLLED ITEMS

Certain things are completely prohibited from being brought into the country or require a licence. Most are obvious but here are a few you might get tripped up on:

➤ Self-defence products such as telescopic truncheons, electric shock devices and self-protection gas canisters. Contact UK Customs National Advice Service: www.hmrc.gov.uk 0845 0109000 or from outside the UK +44 2920 501261– personal phone line advice given Monday-Friday 8am-8pm.

➤ Counterfeit and pirated goods (see below) and goods that infringe patents when brought into the UK such as watches, clocks and CDs and any goods with false marks as to their origin.

➤ Certain animal skins, shells and ivory products as protected under CITES (Convention on International Trade in Endangered Species). All wild birds and animals and most pet birds from outside the EU. Endangered species. Contact DEFRA Global Wildlife Advice: www.defra.gov.uk/wildlife-countryside/gwd/index.htm 01173 728749.

➤ Pets, except those covered by a passport under the Pet Travel Scheme (see Pets).

➤ Certain plants and their products (see below). Contact DEFRA Plant Health Line www.defra.gov.uk/planth/ph.htm 08459 335577.

➤ Certain radio transmitters, such as CB radios and cordless phones not approved for use within the UK (Check with Ofcom: www.ofcom.org.uk 0207 981 3000).

Expert's tip ✦

It is your responsibility to check on whether or not you are allowed to bring certain goods into the UK.

✳ MARKETS ✳

You'll encounter street markets of one type of another everywhere in the world but some are special:

➤ UK: Portobello Road, West Central London – antiques.

➤ Austria: Vienna – Christmas market.

➤ France: Le Marché aux Puces, Saint Ouen, Paris – flea market.

➤ Germany: Nuremberg – Christmas market.

➤ Australia: The Rocks, Sydney – flea market.

➤ USA: The Annexe/Hell's Kitchen, West 39th St between 9th and 10th Ave, New York – flea market.

➤ Israel: Jaffa, Tel Aviv – flea market.

➤ Spain: La Boqueria, Barcelona – covered food market.

➤ China: Temple Street Night Market, Kowloon – clothing, food stalls and outdoor dentistry.

➤ Cambodia: Skuon (70km north of Phnom Penh) – food.

➤ India: New Delhi – spice market.

➤ Egypt: Khan el-Khalili, Cairo – gold, silver and brass.

➤ Ecuador: Otavalo – general market but especially local textiles.

Expert's tip ✦

♦ Watch out for pickpockets (see Security).

♦ Always try haggling (see below), even in countries where negotiation isn't normally expected.

✳ NEGOTIATING ✳

British people don't tend to be very good at this mainly because it's not much practised at home. But getting a bargain can be one of the most rewarding aspects of shopping in some countries abroad. It's not just markets – in countries such as China, India, Indonesia and Egypt haggling is the norm.

Expert's tip ✦

♦ Do research; get to know the average value of your item.

♦ Don't be self-conscious – this is meant to be fun.

♦ Set yourself achievable targets.

♦ Bring cash (but watch out for those pickpockets). Wait until a reduced price has been offered then ask for a further reduction for cash.

♦ Dress down – if you look wealthy the price of the item might start even higher than normal.

♦ Show hesitation about buying your item – get a friend or family member to advise loudly against the purchase.

♦ Be polite and calm.

♦ Be prepared to revisit several times.

♦ Don't forget the old adage – if you don't want it, it's not cheap.

FAKES AND SCAMS

Fakes are huge business the world over. In the UK alone the business is estimated to be worth around £14 million a year, mostly in sunglasses, designer handbags, clothes and watches, while worldwide the trade is now worth £300 billion a year.

There are also pharmaceutical fakes and these can be dangerous to the consumer.

JEWELLERY AND GEMS

Gemstones can be artificially treated to make them appear of higher quality than they are. Look out for:

➤ Coatings. Jasper is often dipped in petrol to bring out its colour. (Try smelling or even tasting it with the tip of your tongue.) Similarly, emeralds are sometimes oiled and turquoise is waxed – you may be able to feel these coatings with your fingers.

➤ Dyes. These are very commonly used. On clear gemstones the dye may be visible in cracks which may be darker than the rest of the stone. Dye can sometimes be detected as a white residue that can be rubbed off. Be particularly wary of lapis, rose quartz, amethyst and citrine.

➤ Paint. The bottom of a gem – most usually a diamond - can be treated with a spot of paint to alter the colour of the whole stone. For instance a yellow diamond may have a spot of purple paint at the bottom to make its appearance clearer (and its value higher). Never buy an expensive piece of jewellery with a closed setting, other than from a reputable jeweller, and always look closely at the bottom of the gem.

➤ Doublets and triplets. These are pieces where two or more gems are glued together for decorative effect. But sometimes a real stone may be mixed with an imitation. This in itself is not illegal as long as you, the buyer, are told. So be sure to ask.

➤ Heat treatment. 'Cooking' gems can temporarily enhance their colour and can be very difficult to spot.

➤ Misnomers. Gems are sometimes called by names that can catch out the unwary. For example, 'Brazilian Diamonds' aren't diamonds at all but topaz.

Frequently used 'misnomers' include:
— American Ruby – garnet
— Brazilian Diamond – colourless topaz
— Ceylon Opal – moonstone
— Brazilian Emerald – green tourmaline
— Indian Emerald – dyed and cracked quartz
— Oriental Amethyst – purple sapphire
— Lavender Jade – dyed howlite
— Spanish Emerald – green glass
— Water Sapphire – iolite

Be sure you understand the difference between the three words – natural, synthetic and imitation:.

➤ Natural – the real thing.

➤ Synthetic – a gem that has the same chemical composition, appearance, lustre and durability as the real thing but which has been made in a laboratory. Synthetics can be made in volume and should be much cheaper than genuine stones.

➤ Imitation – a gem that superficially resembles the real thing but is actually of a very different chemical composition. For example, red glass can resemble a ruby and green glass an emerald. Such imitations are almost worthless.

Expert's tip

♦ Always ask if a stone your're interested in is 'natural', 'synthetic' or 'imitation'.

♦ If it's cheap compared with shop or internet prices then it's either fake or stolen.

♦ Check the quality of the product. Fakes normally use poor quality materials and show little attention to details like hems and seams.

♦ Check the label – if it's badly sewn it's suspicious and a misspelling is an obvious giveaway.

♦ Pay by credit card whenever you can – your credit card company can then take up the matter if something turns out to be a fake.

♦ Keep your eye on your purchases. It has been known for goods to be swapped for something broken or substantially different between payment and wrapping.

✳ SENDING SHOPPING BY POST ✳

Sometimes it's more convenient to send yourself a parcel of your travel purchases rather than carry them back in your luggage. But remember: *many of the duty-free and tax-free advantages only count if you're carrying the goods in person.*

FROM WITHIN THE EU

From within the EU you can send yourself your tax paid purchases by post without having to pay import duty, excise duty or further VAT. But Customs and Excise does insist on the little green slip declaration form being completed accurately. It also maintains the right to check any package at random in the pursuit of drugs or other illegal goods being brought in under the cover of a brown envelope.

FROM OUTSIDE THE EU

Parcels you send yourself from outside the EU may be liable to:

➤ Customs duty – but the customs duty is waived if the amount of duty is less than £7.

➤ Excise duty – charged on tobacco and alcohol *in addition* to customs duty; the rate on wines and spirits is related to alcohol content.

➤ VAT – charged at 17.5% on the purchase price of the items plus duty plus shipping costs, except where the value does not exceed £36.

For full details: www.hmrc.gov.uk 0845 0109000 or + 44 2920 501261.

Expert's tip ✚

If you're sending a number of gifts in one package then, to get the maximum allowance, they should each be individually wrapped and addressed and declared separately on the customs form.

TIME ZONES

Theoretically, time zones extend for 15° of longitude (360° divided by 24 hours). But in reality, zones follow national and physical boundaries rather than lines of longitude.

Officially, the new day starts on the International Date Line, which runs down the Bering Sea, between Russia and Alaska, then to the west of Hawaii and to the east of New Zealand. Which means time travel is possible. It can be Monday to the west of the Line but step (or, more usually, sail or fly) across to the other side and, hey presto, you're back 24 hours and it's Sunday again.

✳ YOUR GUIDE TO TIME ZONES ✳ WORLDWIDE

City	Time difference in hours compared with the UK (GMT)
Accra	0
Anchorage	-9
Athens	+2
Auckland	+12
Bangkok	+7
Berlin	+1
Brussels	+1
Buenos Aires	-3
Cairo	+2
Cape Town	+2
Casablanca	0

City	Time difference in hours compared with the UK (GMT)
Chicago	-6
Delhi	+5h 30 min
Havana	-5
Helsinki	+2
Hong Kong	+8
Honolulu	-10
Los Angeles	-8
Madrid	+1
Mexico City	-6
Miami	-5
Montreal	+5
Moscow	+3
Nairobi	+3
New York	-5
Oslo	+1
Paris	+1
Peking	+8
Perth	+8
Rio de Janeiro	-3
Reykjavik	0
Sydney	+10
Tokyo	+9
Vancouver	-8

Example: When it's noon in London it's +8 hours in Peking = 8pm (20.00); and it's – 5 hours in New York = 7am (07.00).

TRANSPORT

✳ FLYING ✳

Airlines are just the same as other kinds of businesses – if you want to buy one of something you pay the normal price but if you buy 100 you get a special price. Bucket shops or 'travel consolidators' take advantage of this simple rule of economic life.

BUCKET SHOPS

Bucket shops are travel agents that, by buying large numbers of tickets, can sell them on to the public at less than the published fares. They come in several forms:

➤ Destination Specialists – consolidators who, by specialising in particular destinations, can negotiate extremely low prices with the relevant airline or airlines. Sometimes these consolidators sell complete packages including hotel and car hire and make little or nothing on the air fare.

➤ Wholesale Consolidators – companies that sell large numbers of tickets to travel agents rather than direct to the public.

➤ Round The World Consolidators – specialists in round-the-world or multi-stop tickets; if that's what you want, you'll get the best price from a company dedicated to it. Take a look at www.airtreks.com.

➤ Online Travel Consolidators – by eliminating the overheads associated with high street outlets these kinds of companies can offer the very lowest prices. These are the main online companies:

– www.expedia.com – flights, hotels, car hire, cruises, packages.
– www.travelocity.com – flights, hotels, car hire, rail, cruises, packages.
– www.travelsupermarket.com – flights, hotels, car hire, rail, cruises, packages, insurance, airport parking.
– www.skyscanner.net – uses search engine technology to scan airline websites for the best price.
– www.cheapflights.co.uk – specialist in cheap flights from the UK; includes a useful list of telephone numbers to speak to a person at an airline.
– www.statravel.com – for students and those under 26.
– www.dialaflight.com – UK company, established more than 25 years, and offering cheap flights, hotels, car hire, packages, insurance.

Expert's tip ✦

♦ Try to get the minimum number of connections or airline changes – the more there are the more chance there is of something going wrong.

♦ If the ticket is marked 'non-endorsable' it means that, if you miss a connection, you can't be re-routed on another airline.

♦ If you're only flying one-way with a regular airline (for budget airlines, see below) it may sometimes be cheaper to buy a round-trip ticket and throw away the return portion.

♦ When dealing with small bucket shops:
  – Try to use one recommended by someone who had a good experience.
  – Pay with a credit card – if something goes wrong you may be able to get your money back.
  – If possible, collect the ticket in person, rather than have it sent, so you can make sure it's correct.

BUDGET AIRLINES

The low-cost carriers are often criticised but they've done a marvellous job of not only bringing down the cost of flying but also making ticketing conditions more flexible. And although some do, indeed, fly to 'fields in the middle of nowhere' that may well be close to where you want to be.

If you want to know which budget airline flies where try:

➤ http://whichbudget.com
➤ www.low-cost-airline-guide.com

Expert's tip ✦

♦ Some low-cost carriers keep prices within narrow boundaries but others charge vastly different prices depending on the time of year, the day of the week and the time of day.

♦ Generally, the further in advance you book, the cheaper the price.

THE CHEAPEST DAYS

➤ Business routes – high-paying business travellers usually fly on weekdays, especially Mondays and Fridays, so mid-week prices are usually cheaper, with weekend prices the cheapest of all.

➤ Holiday routes – holidaymakers usually fly at weekends so weekday prices (especially mid-week) are usually cheaper.

➤ All routes – it's sometimes cheaper to stay away on a Saturday night.

STANDBY TICKETS

Standby tickets still exist but those *at below the normal fare* have largely disappeared. But they still exist with a few companies such as AirTran Airways in the US, provided you're aged 18 to 22. See www.airtran.com.

HOW TO GET AN UPGRADE

There is no sure way of getting an upgrade other than to pay for it (see below). However, just now and then, passengers do get upgraded, usually because Economy Class is full and the other classes are not. When that happens, your chance of getting the upgrade will be improved if:

➤ You're travelling alone or as a couple and without children.

➤ You are smartly dressed (shirt and tie for a man, dress or business suit for a woman).

➤ You have been polite.

➤ You're a member of a frequent flier programme.

➤ You've persuaded your travel agent to note that you're either SFU (suitable for upgrade) or CIP (commercially important passenger).

Expert's tip ✦

If you happen to be on a flight that's overbooked and volunteer to be 'bumped' then, in compensation, you might be offered a First Class ticket for the next flight.

BUYING AN UPGRADE

Upgrades will normally be charged at the difference between the two classes of fare. However:

➤ Some airlines do sell discounted upgrades *at the airport on the day of departure* when there's space up-front.

➤ Some airlines sell Upgrade Certificates which can then be used to upgrade a confirmed flight on certain routes. Normally you have to call Reservations a day or two before the flight and you'll only get the upgrade if there's space available.

Expert's tip ✦

♦ Upgrade Certificates are relatively cheap but they don't guarantee an upgrade on a specific flight so are only suitable for frequent flyers who have several opportunities to use them. They can often be bought on eBay.

♦ Airlines often have special promotional offers on upgrades and First Class. Watch their websites or see http://firstclass.farecompare.com.

Y-UP

For flights within North America you may be able to purchase a discounted First Class ticket known as a Y-UP. These tickets came about in the 1990s when many companies banned First Class travel for their employees. Y-UP tickets appear to be Coach/Economy class but allow the holder to travel First Class.

➤ Y-UP tickets are not available on all routes or at all times.

➤ Not every airline has a First Class section – check first.

➤ Many Y-UP fares are one-way only.

➤ Remember that Y-Ups only apply to North America.

WARNING: You may see passengers selling their unwanted airline tickets on eBay and other places. Remember that the passenger name on an airline ticket can only be changed if the airline's conditions allow and there may be a substantial administration charge for doing so.

COMFORT

Not all the seats in a class are exactly the same so if you have a choice pick carefully:

➤ Seats by the emergency exits normally have more legroom.

➤ An aisle seat will make it easier to stretch your legs.

➤ A window seat will make it easier to rest your head (and enjoy the view).

➤ A seat in line with the forward part of the wings will move around the least.

Expert's tip ✦

♦ Don't be afraid to bring your own food (subject to security restrictions).

♦ On long-haul flights bring something to entertain you – your own headphones if you like quality sound, an inflatable cushion, an eyemask and a toothbrush. Move around and drink plenty of water (see Health).

♦ For all kinds of useful airline information from seat pitches to check-in procedures see www.seatguru.com.

AIRPORT PARKING

There are three styles of parking:

➤ On-airport – the closest and most expensive.

➤ Off-airport – the cheapest, but you'll then have to transfer by dedicated bus.

➤ Meet and greet – you drive to a pick-up point at the airport, unload, and your car is then driven away to be parked. On your return your car is delivered back to the pick-up point. It's expensive but may be less than the standard short-term on-airport rate.

Always get prices from several companies as rates may vary significantly:

➤ www.airparks.co.uk
➤ www.aph.com

➢ www.fhr-net.co.uk
➢ www.holidayextras.co.uk
➢ www.parkbcp.co.uk
➢ www.parking4less.co.uk
➢ www.purpleparking.com
➢ www.simplyparking.co.uk

Expert's tip ✦

Book as far in advance as possible to get the cheapest prices – savings in advance off-airport can be as much as 60% of the on-airport price.

AIRPORT HOTEL/PARKING COMBINATIONS

If you have an early flight, booking an airport hotel for the night before could relieve both your stress and your parking problems. Many of the same companies that offer airport parking also offer hotel/parking combinations (Airparks, APH, BCP, FHR and Holiday Extras – see above); in addition you might like to try:

➢ www.simply-hotels.co.uk
➢ www.superbreak.com

Expert's tip ✦

♦ *Before booking a hotel/parking combination, check not just the transfer time to the terminal but also that the hotel operates a shuttle when you need it.*

♦ *Book as far in advance as possible to get the best price.*

UNACCOMPANIED CHILDREN

Different airlines have different policies about children flying alone:

➤ Budget airlines generally won't accept unaccompanied minors under 14.

➤ 'Normal' airlines will generally accept unaccompanied minors from the age of five for single-sector direct non-stop flights, and six for longer flights. There's usually an additional charge for the extra supervision. The age at which children *don't* have to register as unaccompanied minors is generally around 12.

In either case, the minimum age for accompanying a young child is generally 16 – so, for example, a daughter of 16 could accompany her brother aged 10.

Make sure your child knows what to do if:

➤ Luggage is lost or damaged

➤ The flight is delayed or diverted or cancelled

➤ Something is stolen. (Impress on your child the need to be vigilant at the baggage carousel – that's often the moment when hand-baggage disappears.)

Make sure your child has:

➤ Enough money for food and drinks.

➤ A mobile phone, a phone card or enough change to make phone calls.

➤ Any medicines he or she needs.

Expert's tip ✛

♦ Always stay at the airport until your child's flight has taken off.

♦ Find out the airline's policy on overnight accommodation in the case of, say, the flight being diverted

LUGGAGE

SHOULD I LOCK MY BAG?

Airlines recommend passengers to lock bags. But bear in mind that if security personnel wish to carry out a hand search they may break the lock. For more on this see the section on Security.

LOST LUGGAGE

A typical figure is that for every thousand airline customers, six or seven bags won't make it to the baggage carousel when they should. Some well-known airlines even have figures as high as 20.

But, fortunately, only about 0.005% of air passengers' luggage is *never* reunited with its owners – that's about one bag in 20,000. Of course, the figure would be even smaller if everyone put clear contact details on their cases. In the future a tiny computer chip will probably be embedded in your luggage tag so that, using Radio Frequency Identification (RFID) airlines will always be able to match owners with their property. In the meantime, to make sure baggage that's been delayed or lost will be delivered to you by courier:

➤ Put your name, address and telephone number inside each case.

➤ Put your name and mobile telephone number on the outside and, if possible, an address other than your home address, such as the hotel you're travelling to. (The idea is that a professional burglar won't be alerted to your absence from home.)

➤ If you're travelling to various destinations also include a copy of your itinerary so airline staff will know where to forward your cases.

Remember, it's not just airlines that lose luggage. Passengers are also quite good at it. At Heathrow, for example, around 120 passengers forget their laptops every month and about 15 never make any attempt to reclaim them.

UNACCOMPANIED LUGGAGE

Some airlines will let you send your luggage unaccompanied. If you have a lot, compare the price with the excess baggage charge.

➤ You must hold an international ticket for travel between the two points.

➤ Your luggage may only contain personal clothing and effects.

Alternatively, you can pay a company to forward your luggage to your destination address. That means you don't have to lug bags to the airport, wait to check them in, or wait at the baggage carousel at the other end. (But forwarding companies will only collect your bags within a certain radius of the airport.) It's not cheap but it is convenient. Put 'luggage forwarding' and the name of the country you're in into your search engine or see:

➤ www.carrymyluggage.com 0845 009 0362 – UK

➤ www.directbaggage.com 0116 287 5269 – UK

➤ www.luggageforward.com 00 1 617 482 1100 (international number for US company)

➤ www.luggagefree.com 00 1 212 453 1579

Expert's tip ✛

♦ Put your name and address on as many things as possible – clothing, cameras, electronic goods, glasses.

♦ Make an inventory of the main items in your case.

♦ Don't overfill suitcases – they might burst open with the sort of rough handling they sometimes get.

- ◆ *Distinguish your bag from similar ones by, say, putting a ribbon through the handle or, better still, using a luggage strap; a luggage strap will also protect against accidental opening.*
- ◆ *If you're issued with bar codes for your checked luggage, keep them in a safe place – they're the proof that your luggage was, indeed, checked in.*
- ◆ *Make sure your luggage is clearly marked with your name on the outside and your name and contact details on the inside.*
- ◆ *Keep vital documents and medicines in your hand luggage.*
- ◆ *If your luggage isn't delivered to the carousel, immediately report the matter to the baggage agent on duty and fill in the appropriate forms.*

WHAT HAPPENS TO LOST LUGGAGE?

Amazingly, some people never do reclaim their luggage – or, at least, not successfully. Then what happens? In America, after at least 90 days, the airlines may sell it. A company called Unclaimed Baggage has turned it into a business, handling more than a million items a year. See www.unclaimedbaggage.com.

In the UK a lot of unclaimed airline baggage (as well as from Transport for London) is sold on Tuesdays by Greasby's Auction House in Tooting Broadway, South London, with the proceeds going to charity. See www.greasbys.co.uk 020 8672 2972 or 020 8682 4564.

AIRPORT LOUNGES

If you have a long wait before a flight, and especially if you want to get on with work, an airport lounge is the solution. Many airlines have their own, available to passengers paying higher fares (for example, British Airways customers in First, Club World, Club Europe, plus Silver and Gold Executive Club). But you can also enjoy the facilities of an exclusive lounge (comfort, tranquillity, refreshments, telephones, internet access) simply by paying.

Prices vary depending on the airport, the lounge, the day, the time and the demand but are generally from £13.50 to £20 per person with a maximum stay of three hours. For the best deal, compare prices:

➤ www.executivelounges.com
➤ www.holidayextras.co.uk
➤ www.loungepass.com
➤ www.simplylounges.co.uk

Expert's tip ✛

As a member of www.prioritypass.com you can enjoy free access to airport lounges all over the world, but you'll need to fly more than 20 times a year to make it worthwhile. Members of Diner's Club have free access to over 100 airport lounges worldwide – but none of them are in the UK.

AIRPORT TRANSFERS

You've booked your flight on the internet and you've booked your hotel the same way. But how do you get to it from the airport? You could just hope to find a convenient bus on arrival or queue for a taxi. But there is another way. You can be sure of your transfer if you *pre-book* either:

➤ A private transfer. Always possible. You'll be met at arrivals (or told to proceed to a pick-up point) and the vehicle will be for you only. Note that cost is normally based on the vehicle rather than a per-person charge.

➤ A shuttle transfer. Only available where and when there's sufficient demand. You'll be directed to a pick-up point from which shuttles will depart at fixed times to a variety of destinations. Obviously you'll be sharing the shuttle with other people and charged per-person.

For further information:

➤ www.a2btransfers.com – No telephone
➤ www.a-t-s.net 0709 209 7392
➤ www.holidaytaxis.com 01444 257 041
➤ www.resorthoppa.com 0871 855 0350
➤ www.transfer-intelligence.com 0871 666 0754
➤ www.transferstore.com 0870 811 0066

✳ FERRIES AND THE ✳ CHANNEL TUNNEL

There are more than a score of ways of escaping from Britain by ferry. Here they are.

To: Belgium
➤ Hull – Zeebrugge
➤ Ramsgate – Ostend
➤ Rosyth – Zeebrugge

To: Denmark
➤ Harwich – Esbjerg

To: France
➤ Dover – Boulogne
➤ Dover – Calais
➤ Dover – Dunkerque
➤ Folkestone – Calais
➤ Newhaven – Dieppe
➤ Newhaven – Le Havre
➤ Plymouth – Roscoff
➤ Plymouth – St Malo
➤ Poole – Cherbourg
➤ Poole – St Malo
➤ Portsmouth – Caen
➤ Portsmouth – Cherbourg

➤ Portsmouth – Le Havre
➤ Portsmouth – St Malo

To: Holland
➤ Harwich – Hook Of Holland
➤ Hull – Rotterdam
➤ Newcastle – Amsterdam

To: Ireland
➤ Fishguard – Rosslare
➤ Holyhead – Dublin
➤ Holyhead – Dun Laoghaire
➤ Liverpool – Dublin
➤ Pembroke – Rosslare
➤ Swansea – Cork

To: Norway
➤ Newcastle – Bergen

To: Spain
➤ Portsmouth – Bilbao
➤ Plymouth – Santander

You can book directly with the companies or by using one of the online ferry specialists:

➤ www.cheapferrytickets.com
➤ www.ferrybooker.com
➤ www.ferries.co.uk

Expert's tip

Register online with one of the ferry booking specialists or with the relevant ferry operator to receive immediate details of special offers by e-mail. On Ferrybooker (see above) you can just click on 'Special Offers'.

If you want to take your pet on a ferry see Pets. If you want to take your bike on a ferry each company has its own policy and price structure but you shouldn't encounter any problems.

THE CHANNEL TUNNEL

www.eurotunnel.com 0800 969 992 (UK) or 0800 800 474 (France) – website for taking your car through the Channel Tunnel. You don't have to book in advance but by reserving you make sure of your place. On the other hand, if you reserve a standard ticket and are more than 24 hours late you lose your money. There can be a big difference in price between standard tickets and so-called FlexiPlus fares which allow you to amend your ticket. For the cheapest price:

➤ Look on the website for the cheapest times (they're not necessarily what you might imagine).

➤ Buy a standard ticket.

➤ Book well in advance.

➤ Don't be late.

www.eurostar.com 08705 186 186 (UK) or 00 44 1233 617 575 (from abroad) – website for foot passengers travelling through the Channel Tunnel by train. If you want a little luxury opt for the dedicated Leisure Select or Business Premier compartments, but for the cheapest deals:

➤ Use the 'availability calendar' to spot the cheapest prices.

➤ Buy a non-flexible ticket.

➤ Book well in advance.

Don't miss your train because a non-flexible ticket can't be either exchanged or refunded.

✳ CRUISES ✳

Cruising has traditionally been very expensive and still can be. But there are bargains to be had if you cruise off-season or take advantage of last-minute deals and promotions. Put 'cheap cruises' into your search engine, together with the cruising area you want, or see:

➤ www.the-psa.co.uk – website of the Passenger Shipping Association which represents cruise and ferry companies selling products in the UK. 020 7436 2449.

➤ www.cabincloseouts.com – discount cruises.

➤ www.cruisecheap.com – special deals on cruises.

➤ www.vacationstogo.com – listings of last-minute cruise reductions and special promotions.

➤ www.easycruise.com 0871 210 0001 – the 'easy' formula comes to cruising the Greek islands.

SAILING AS CREW

Quite large numbers of people need to move a yacht from A to B (usually from the Med to the Caribbean or back) and are just too busy making money to do it themselves. And those yachts need crews. It helps if you actually know how to sail but as long as you're capable of following some simple instructions and appear to be a congenial sort of companion you have a chance if you register with:

➤ www.crewseekers.co.uk 01489 578 319
➤ www.pydww.com 01539 552 130
➤ www.reliance-yacht.com 01252 378 239

You can also pay for a passage aboard a tall ship. Yes, they still exist as commercial vessels. Take a look at www.classic-sailing.co.uk and you'll see for yourself (01872 580 022). Of course, these ships aren't plying back and forth on a regular basis but if you're in no particular hurry you should be able to find a crossing to suit.

✳ COACHES ✳

Unless you're a businessman in a hurry, there's almost nowhere in the UK that can't reasonably be reached by coach. Coach is also a practical proposition for most journeys in Europe. Let's say you want to go to the French Alps for a spot of cross-country skiing. You could get a coach leaving London at teatime and be in your resort at lunchtime the following day. That's not bad.

Europe's largest coach network is Eurolines. It actually comprises 32 independent coach companies all collaborating to cover some 500 destinations as far away as Moscow and Morocco.

➤ To find out how to get around on public transport in the UK take a look at: www.traveline.org.uk 0871 200 22 33 (charged at 10p per minute from a BT landline).

➤ For an itinerary on train, coach (or, indeed, car) see: www.transportdirect.info.

➤ For National Express see www.nationalexpress.com 08705 80 80 80.

➤ For Eurolines see www.nationalexpress.com/eurolines 08705 80 80 80.

➤ For Stagecoach see www.nationalexpress.com or telephone Traveline (see above).

BIKES BY COACH

European Bike Express operates within the UK and to France, Spain and Italy, using trailers specially equipped for bicycles.

There are four routes. Within the UK the service runs from Thornaby via various large towns to Folkestone. Then from Calais there's a service to Agen (France), another to Ampuriabrava (Spain – Costa Brava) and lastly to Cavallino (Italy). You can return from your drop-off point (usually 17 days later) or you can cycle to a different pick up.

➤ www.bike-express.co.uk 01430 422 111

THE WORLD'S LONGEST REGULAR COACH SERVICE

Step aboard OzBus in London and you can step off 12 weeks and 15,000 miles (24,000 km) later close to Sydney Opera House. The price is a little bit more than the typical flight at £3,750. But when you consider that it's spread over 84 nights and includes food and accommodation in tents and budget hotels (with a few nights sitting up in the coach) it's pretty good value at around £45 a day.

➤ www.oz-bus.com 0208 641 1443

Several OzBus clients have published blogs. See http://ozbus diaries.blogspot.com or just put OzBus into your search engine and see what you can find.

✳ TRAINS ✳

CHEAP TRAIN TICKETS

Before you buy a train ticket you need to do a little research. Take a look at:

➤ www.moneysavingexpert.com
➤ www.thetrainline.com
➤ www.internationaltrainline.com

Next, consider a Railcard. Railcards come in five categories:

➤ Young Person's Railcard. Ages 16-25 (26 if you're in full-time education). Saving: one-third. Cost £20.

➤ Family Railcard. For up to four adults and four children (5 to 15). You don't have to be related. Saving: one-third on adult fares, 60% on children's fares. Cost £20.

➤ Senior Railcard. For those 60 or over. Saving: one-third. Cost £20.

➤ Network Railcard. For those travelling for leisure in South-East England. Saving: one-third on adult fares, 60% on children's fares. Cost £20.

➤ Disabled Person's Railcard. If you're disabled you and one adult can save one-third of the fare. Cost £18 (£48 for three years).

It comes down to this. If you're making just one trip and the ticket costs more than £60 it's worth getting a Railcard. If you're travelling frequently by train it's essential. Note there are some restrictions but if you don't have to get somewhere early you'll probably be able to claim your discount.

FIRST-CLASS TICKETS

First-class rail tickets certainly don't have the sort of premium you'd have to pay on a plane. Different companies have different policies but, in general, the longer you book in advance the cheaper the first-class ticket is likely to be. Most companies operate a three-tier structure. When the cheapest is sold out so the price jumps to the next level.

In reality, the cheap standard-class tickets tend to sell out quickest. Which means that when standard tickets have jumped up to the middle price, first-class tickets may still be at the cheapest level. And the price difference may then be quite small. In some cases, the extra cost of first-class can be as little as 15%. At weekends, when business travellers are at home, upgrading to first-class can be a real bargain. It can add as little as £10 to the cost of a ticket from London to Birmingham and just £20 to the cost of getting to Glasgow.

EUROSTAR

See The Channel Tunnel above.

Expert's tip ✦

Getting all the necessary information for a complicated train journey abroad has been solved for you by one Mark Smith who, as a hobby, has set up a website called The Man In Seat Sixty-One. Quite frankly, it beats the operators' official websites hands down. You want to know how to get to Morocco by train? He'll give you every detail. The Far East? No problem. He's not even daunted by Australia. The answer to just about every question you ever thought of is here:

♦ www.seat61.com

BIKES ON TRAINS

Now that Britain's railways are run by various different companies there's no uniform policy on bicycles in the UK, except that under the National Conditions of Carriage operators *aren't* obliged to carry them. You'll have to contact each company individually. But, generally, there's not too much problem. As regards the Channel Tunnel, you and your bicycle will be loaded onto a special minibus and from there onto Eurostar.

✳ HIGH-TECH HITCHHIKING ✳

Rather than stand beside the road with your thumb out, simply go to www.freewheelers.com, register on the site, enter the details of your proposed journey (as far in advance as possible) and wait for someone to contact you. If they like the sound of you they offer you a lift on a cost-sharing basis. It's a simple idea that's already well-established in Germany (they call it *Mitzfahrzentralen*), France (*Autostop*), Belgium (*Taxistop*) and Switzerland (*Sharcom*). Freewheelers is free but does ask for donations.

WEATHER

Finding out about the weather anywhere in the world has never been easier, provided you have access to the internet. Here are some sites on which you can get forecasts:

GENERAL FORECASTS

➤ http://ukweather.com – UK and international weather.

➤ www.bbc.co.uk/weather/ – Current conditions and forecasts for the UK and the world.

➤ www.metoffice.gov.uk/weather

➤ www.accuweather.com – Forecasts for the USA and the world.

➤ www.wunderground.com – Weather in the USA and world, with good graphics, maps and radar images.

➤ www.weather.com – Good for weather in the USA.

➤ www.nws.noaa.gov/ – Official US weather forecasts, including for aviation and shipping, as well as details of any fires.

SHIPPING FORECASTS

➤ www.metoffice.gov.uk/weather/marine/shipping_forecast.html

UV REPORTS

Weather reports and forecasts often include an index of ultra-violet radiation from the sun. The higher the index the greater the danger (see Health). The clearer the sky, the higher the altitude, the closer to the equator, the closer to mid-summer and the closer to mid-day the greater the UV Index will be. Risks will be intensified by snow or water which reflect the sun's rays.

UV Index	Recommendation
0 – 2	Precautions only necessary if you're fair skinned or in snow
3 – 5	Wear sunglasses and a hat
6 – 7	High risk of harm. Wear sunglasses, a hat and keep covered up. Keep out of the sun from mid-morning until mid-afternoon.
8 – 10	Very high risk. Take the same precautions as for UV 6 – 7 but be even more vigilant.
11+	Extreme risk.

For more on the hazards of UV rays see Health.

SNOW REPORTS

Theoretically you can ski somewhere in the world every day of the year. The dates given below are for the resorts with the best snow records, due to their favourable geography. Resorts at low altitudes or with less favourable geography may have considerably shorter seasons.

➤ Alps: November – May
➤ Australia/New Zealand: July – October
➤ Canada (Rockies): November – May
➤ Canada (Quebec): December – March
➤ Japan: December – May
➤ South America: June – October

➤ USA (Rockies): November – May

➤ USA (New England): December – March.

Here are some useful websites (and don't forget the webcams as explained below and in the chapter on Researching And Exploring):

➤ www.ifyouski.com/snow/snow/ – weather and ski resort information worldwide.

➤ www.skiclub.co.uk – current snow conditions and forecasts for some 250 ski resorts.

➤ www.onthesnow.com – hourly snow and weather conditions for some 2,000 ski resorts worldwide.

➤ www.snow-forecast.com – forecasts for different altitudes within the resort network. Six-day forecasts free; nine-day forecasts for subscribers only.

WHEN TO GO, WHEN NOT TO GO

MONSOONS AND RAINY SEASONS

The monsoon season is a difficult time in south-Asia. There's also a monsoon season in North America, although far less problematic.

➤ South-east Asia and Australasia – December to March

➤ South-west Asia including India – June to September

➤ North-America – July to September

The rainy season in the Caribbean runs from May to December, overlapping the hurricane season (see below) but mostly it's a matter of brief showers.

HURRICANES

The Caribbean, Mexico, Florida and Texas suffer a hurricane season that runs from June to November, peaking in the months of August to October. However, while there's a certainty of lower prices, on the other hand there's no guarantee of hurricanes. You could easily spend two weeks there without even experiencing high winds. Safest islands are considered to be Aruba, Bonaire and Curacao.

For detailed information see: www.stormcarib.com

Expert's tip ✦

If you're planning a holiday in the Caribbean during the hurricane season look for resorts that give a weather guarantee.

WEATHER ALERTS

If you're a frequent traveller and you'd like to be able to see at a glance if there are any weather problems anywhere in Europe then go to:

➢ www.meteoalarm.eu/

Meteoalarm is a collaboration between more than 20 European national weather services and its opening graphic immediately shows if there's a problem. It could be extreme heat, extreme cold, snow, avalanche danger and many other things.

➢ White   Insufficient information
➢ Green   No particular problem
➢ Yellow   Weather is potentially dangerous
➢ Orange   Weather is dangerous
➢ Red   Weather is very dangerous

✳ THE WEATHER RIGHT NOW ✳

If you want to know what the weather is like *right now* the best thing you can do is to search out a webcam as close as possible to the relevant destination. The numbers are growing all the time, especially in tourist areas.

Let's say it's Thursday morning and you're wondering where to go for a weekend's skiing. Just put the name of a ski resort and the word 'webcam' into your search engine and see what comes up. If there's a webcam you'll be able to see for yourself what the weather is like and how much snow there is.

Expert's tip ✦

When viewing a webcam image from a ski resort pay particular attention to key indicators such as the amount of snow on roofs and trees. The depth of snow on roofs suggests the depth of snow on the piste. A lot of snow on trees suggests a recent snowfall and cold weather; trees bare of snow suggests no recent snowfall and/or warm weather.

For more on webcams see Researching And Exploring.

GLOSSARY OF TRAVEL INDUSTRY TERMS

ABTA – Association of British Travel Agents

a la carte – you can choose any dishes and each will be priced separately.

AP – American Plan. The hotel price includes three meals a day (but not usually wine or cocktails), also known as Full Pension or Full Board.

Back to back ticketing – taking advantage of the fact that trips that include a Saturday night are often cheaper. Let's say, for example, you wish to fly to Destination A on Monday and return on Thursday. Because no Saturday night is involved the ticket is expensive. So, instead, you buy a cheap round-trip excursion to Destination A, departing Monday and including a Saturday night; in addition, you buy a second round-trip excursion from Destination A, departing Thursday and also including a Saturday night.

Bait and switch – an American term for the practice of advertising a low price and then telling customers the tickets are sold out in the hope of selling them more expensive tickets.

BALPA – British Airline Pilots Association

CAA – Civil Aviation Authority

Cabotage – Flights between two points within a country, usually denied to carriers from other countries.

Cancellation Penalty – the amount you'll have to pay if you cancel your booking.

Coach – on an aircraft, the American term for Economy Class.

Code Sharing – an agreement whereby one airline allows another to use its code in its flight schedule display.

Computerised Reservation System (CRS) – old-fashioned term for Global Distribution System (GDS).

Continental Breakfast – a light breakfast of rolls/croissants, jam, and tea or coffee.

Corporate Rate – a reduced rate a hotel charges regular business customers.

Coupon Broker – a person who illegally buys and resells Frequent Flyer Awards.

Cross-Border Ticketing – issuing an air ticket that makes it seem the journey began in a country where prices are cheaper.

Curbside Check-In – a service that allows passengers to check their bags outside the terminal building.

Demi-pension – half-board (that is, breakfast and evening meal).

Dine-Around Plan – when paying full or half-board you have a choice of restaurants.

Double Occupancy Rate – the price charged when two people occupy a room.

Drop-Off Charge – an extra fee for leaving a hire car at a different location from the one where you collected it.

Economy Plus – on an aircraft, an intermediate class between Coach and Business Class, with additional legroom and other benefits.

Electronic Ticketing – system used by airlines where information is held on computer and a paper ticket isn't required.

EP – European Plan. The hotel price excludes meals.

English Breakfast – a substantial cooked breakfast usually including a choice of eggs, bacon and sausages as well as cereal, fruit juice and beverages.

Entrée – the main course

Excess Baggage – luggage that exceeds the allowed weight, dimensions or number of pieces.

Excursion Fare – a fare that, because of certain restrictions, is cheaper than the standard fare.

Familymoon – like a honeymoon but for a second or subsequent wedding, with children or other family members included.

Feeder Airline – a local carrier on which people fly into a major airport to transfer to a major carrier.

Fifth Freedom – the freedom (often denied) of an airline to carry passengers between two foreign destinations.

Fly-Drive Package – a travel package that includes air travel and car hire and, sometimes, accommodation as well.

Force Majeure – an event that could not be anticipated or controlled and for which the supplier (airline, hotel, travel agent etc.) cannot be held legally responsible.

Front-Line Agent – an agent who deals directly with the public.

Fuel Surcharge – an additional fee charged on top of the ticket price to cover the rising cost of fuel.

Galileo – A computerised reservation system.

Gemini – Another computerised reservation system.

Global Distribution System (GDS) – an international comp-uter reservation system that embraces the reservation databases of several companies.

Ground Operator – a company that provides such services as transfers and coach tours for incoming clients.

Half Pension – half-board (that is, breakfast and evening meal).

High Season – the most popular period when prices are at their most expensive.

Hub-And-Spoke – a way of organising aircraft so that long-dis-tance passengers fly into a centre (the hub) and then transfer to smaller aircraft to reach their final destinations.

IAPA – International Air Passenger Association.

IATA – International Air Transport Association.

ICAO – International Civil Aviation Organization.

Involuntary Denied Boarding – the airline term for being 'bumped' from a flight; in other words, the flight is overbooked.

IT Fare – inclusive tour fare.

Jumpseat – the fold-down seat used by flight attendants.

Late-Booking Fee – an extra charge made when someone books a holiday at the last minute.

Liability Waiver – a contract that absolves the supplier of responsibility if something goes wrong; for example, you might be asked to sign a liability waiver if undertaking an extreme sport.

MAP – Modified American Plan. The hotel price includes breakfast and one other meal (usually dinner).

Menu – in Britain asking for the menu means you'd like to dine *à la carte*. But in many countries it means the opposite – that you'd like the set meal.

Metroliner – a fast Amtrak train running between New York and Washington.

Off-Peak/Off-Season – the least popular time of year when prices are at their lowest.

Open Ticket – an air ticket that doesn't specify dates, times or flight numbers.

Overbooking – the practice of accepting more reservations than there's room for, on the basis that there will be 'no shows', that is, a percentage of people who won't turn up.

Pax – passengers.

Rack Rate – the standard price for a hotel room, before any discount.

Red Book – any Michelin guide to hotels and restaurants (because they have red covers, whereas the travel guides have green covers).

Revalidation Sticker – a self-adhesive form stuck to an airline ticket and showing a change of information, such as the date, time or class.

Sabre – a global distribution system (GDS) used by hotels.

Schengen Agreement – named after the town in Belgium where the 'open borders' agreement was signed. The Schengen countries, between which there are no border controls, are: (from within the EU) Austria, Belgium, Czech Republic, Denmark, Estonia, Finland, France, Germany, Greece, Hungary, Italy, Latvia, Lithuania, Luxembourg, Malta, the Netherlands, Poland, Portugal, Slovakia, Slovenia, Spain, Sweden; (from outside the EU) Iceland, Norway.

Scheduled Carrier – an airline that operates in accordance with a regular timetable.

Shoulder Season – period between the high and low seasons with intermediate prices.

Split Ticketing – creating two tickets for a single journey, with the aim of saving money.

Table d'Hôte – fixed-price meal with limited choice, normally at a small hotel.

Ticketless Travel – the same as electronic ticketing.

Travel Advisory – a formal warning, issued at government level, that travel to a destination is dangerous.

Unbundling – charging separately for products or services that used to be included under a single price. For example, charging for an in-flight meal would be unbundling.

Unrestricted Fare – a ticket that, for a higher price, offers maximum flexibility. For example, an unrestricted airline fare wouldn't require an advance purchase period or a Saturday night stay.

Wagon-lits – European company providing a sleeping-car service on trains.

Worldspan – a computerised reservation system.

WTO – World Tourism Organization

Xbag – Excess baggage

✳ CONTACT US ✳

You're welcome to contact White Ladder Press if you have any questions or comments for either us or the authors. Please use whichever of the following routes suits you.

Phone: 0208 334 1600

Email: enquiries@whiteladderpress.com

Fax: 0208 334 1601

Address: 2nd Floor, Westminster House, Kew Road, Richmond, Surrey TW9 2ND

Website: www.whiteladderpress.com

✳ WHAT CAN OUR WEBSITE DO ✳ FOR YOU?

If you want more information about any of our books, you'll find it at **www.whiteladderpress.com.** In particular you'll find extracts from each of our books, and reviews of those that are already published. We also run special offers on future titles if you order online before publication. And you can request a copy of our free catalogue.

Many of our books have links pages, useful addresses and so on relevant to the subject of the book. You'll also find out a bit more about us and, if you're a writer yourself, you'll find our submission guidelines for authors. So please check us out and let us know if you have any comments, questions or suggestions.

INDEX